MW00913202

BE A GLOBAL FORCE OF ONE!™

IN YOUR HOMETOWN

Community

Individual   Schools K-12

Business

**202 Common Sense, Human & Portable Ways
To Restore Our Communities, Our Schools & Ourselves**

by
John T. Boal

PacRim Publishing • Burbank, CA

ii   *Be A Global Force of One! ...*

BE A GLOBAL FORCE OF ONE! ... In Your Hometown

Copyright ©1998 by John T. Boal
All rights reserved.

Every effort was made to check and re-check the accuracy of the information in this book. The primary goal of the contents is to inspire readers to initiate or adapt these programs into their communities or school districts. It is hoped that readers will act in a responsible manner and not take advantage of those resources that offer complimentary materials as many of these are generated by nonprofit organizations. Similar results of these successful programs cannot be guaranteed. Their success will depend on the personal ownership and motivation of those who decide to pursue them.

AUTHOR & PUBLISHER

John T. Boal	Ph:	818-848-2376
PacRim Publishing	Fax:	818-848-7021
150 S. Glenoaks Blvd.,	E-mail:	75322.255@compuserve.com
Ste. 8054		
Burbank, CA 91502		

ORDERING
To order additional copies, contact

Wescom Graphics Inc.	Ph:	818-954-9549, ext. 21
2807 W. Magnolia Blvd.	Fax:	818-954-0498
Burbank, CA 91505		

ISBN   0-9626617-2-4 softcover

CREDITS

Design & Production	Linda Burrows
Front Cover Image	© Chase Swift, compliments of Westlight Stock Photography (800-ART-BUYER)
Printer	Moore Bergstrom Co., Inc.
Paper	100% recycled with soy-based ink

FIRST EDITION
March, 1998

DEDICATION

In memory of

Roberto Clemente

Pittsburgh Pirates 1955-1972

A compassionate humanitarian who also happened to be the greatest rightfielder in the history of baseball.

As one who wore his first baseball uniform at age 3; who slept with his glove under his pillow; who loved the taste of dirt while diving to stop a ball; who tiptoed around Forbes Field in the 1960s like it was a shrine; who dutifully attended the last 14 games at the revered ballpark and, unfortunately, as one whose bat could never figure out the physics of a curveball, I did the next best thing to keep my flame for the game alive.

I became a beer vendor at Three Rivers Stadium when it opened in July, 1970.

During the 1972 season, Roberto's last, I was returning to the commissary for another load of beer when Clemente was getting up from a table where he was signing autographs.

As I approached, our eyes locked and I spoke briefly to him in Spanish as to how he was feeling today. In that moment, Roberto — with supernatural forces of explosive energy and extreme dignity emanating from his compact body — focused all of his concern on me, a lowly beer vendor, and respectfully asked in return how I was doing.

There was not one hint of condescension, just Roberto's singular concentration for a fellow human being that pierced through me like a laser beam. It was a moment in time that has transcended throughout my life. Yet I was by no means alone.

"A lot of people misinterpreted his pride as arrogance," explained Luis Mayoral-Rodriquez, a liaison for Latin American ballplayers, in *In Pittsburgh Weekly*. "They never knew the real Clemente. They knew the sports figure. They didn't know his heart. Roberto identified with the struggler — the poor man, the taxi driver and the factory worker. The people who have to suffer, he used to say, the people who have to work."

Despite Roberto's incredibly acrobatic ability for running down fly balls in the gap; his low-slung "basket catches;" his unequaled cannon arm; his flailing, all out baserunning style and his beloved, 36-ounce knobless bat with his ferocious, helmet-spinning corkscrew swing, his greatest and lasting memory is what he selflessly accomplished and showed by example off the diamond.

Throughout his stellar 18-year career, Roberto continually helped people wherever he was — on Pittsburgh's Hill District where he doled out money to homeless people — or on the streets throughout Puerto Rico where he passed out 50-cent pieces to kids.

Although he was fiercely passionate about his exceptional ability, his heritage and his parents, Roberto didn't fit the traditional mold of a predominantly Anglo-Saxon society that controlled the American pastime and was often unjustly maligned by baseball writers, fans, opponents and teammates. Being black, Latin, stylish, volatile and outspoken were all subtly woven into a web of wicked denigration of his true character. Regardless of how well Roberto played and truly dominated his position for so many years, a lack of understanding by the superficial "opinion makers" who neglected to learn what lay deep within the soul of this courageous man led to a lack of mainstream acceptance.

When the Pirates won the 1960 World Series on Bill Mazeroski's dramatic homerun in the 7th Game, Roberto was again criticized because he didn't celebrate with his teammates and the official city dignitaries. Instead the sweetly innocent Roberto rejoiced in his own special way. He was out in the streets around Schenley Park with the common man and the fans from right field who had faithfully supported him through his early years.

Then on September 30, 1972, the 38-year-old Clemente stroked his 3000th hit, a double off the left-center field wall. I remember it well. I was carrying a load of Iron City beer with my left arm and raising my right fist into the air whooping it up with the rest of the slim crowd. That was Roberto's last hit which in retrospect became all too eerily symmetrical and memorable as it capped his illustrious career.

Two months later, "Clemente woke up one morning and told his wife

(Vera) he'd seen his own funeral in a dream," chronicled Kenneth A. Brown in *In Pittsburgh Weekly.* "Later that month, he went to Nicaragua to manage Puerto Rico's team in the World Series of amateur baseball. He befriended a 14-year-old legless orphan, making arrangements for him to be fitted with artificial legs.

"Two days before Christmas, an earthquake leveled Nicaragua's capital of Managua. Clemente immediately signed on as honorary chair of the island's Nicaraguan Relief Committee. He worked to gather food and supplies, filming TV spots and making calls — even going door-to-door to solicit donations. While his family entertained guests and his Christmas presents lay unopened beneath the tree, Clemente was at the airport loading planes."

In all, he worked 14-hour days and went without sleeping or eating to gather 150 tons of relief supplies for a country where 7000 had been killed and 200,000 were homeless.

Despite the protests of his wife and his best buddies, Manny Sanguillen and Jose Pagan, Clemente was determined to complete his mission of mercy because he feared the rebels in Nicaragua would confiscate the shipment. When asked why he had to leave on New Year's Eve, Clemente simply responded, "For me, every day is the same."

So that night — when most people of such professional stature are busy planning for a gala party — Clemente and 4 others boarded a haphazardly-loaded, previously grounded DC-7. It took off and crashed into the Atlantic Ocean at 9:22 p.m. sending everyone to their premature deaths.

That New Year's Eve, back in Pittsburgh, I had left my radio on all night to a soft music station. For some strange reason, I awoke at 4 a.m. just as the first news of his death was being broadcast. Stunned, I can only remember those next couple days as a blur of community grief throughout Pittsburgh.

It was just 91 days after his 3000th hit and only a month after he foresaw his death in a dream. But just as he played the game, Roberto's passing was not only dramatic but it made a statement as well.

It's a statement that has quietly spread during the 25 years since his heroic effort as dozens of schools, hospitals, health centers, ball fields, parks and streets have all been named in his honor not only around the U.S. but throughout the world.

As just one example of his widespread popularity, in Chicago, a modern, 8-story high school with exceptional physical and educational facilities opened its doors in June, 1974 as Roberto Clemente High School.

Explaining the name change, the school declared, "This extraordinary man is remembered by most people as one who gave all he had to give, including his life, to help his fellow man."

In addition, a U.S. commemorative stamp, a fleet thoroughbred of former Pirates' owner John Galbreath named "Roberto" and the first ballplayer to enter the Hall of Fame before the mandatory 5-year waiting period all add to the legend of one who had such style and substance.

Yet while baseball fans marveled at the exterior Clemente — his awesome physical skills — his enduring legacy is the interior Clemente who as an humanitarian was, and still is, symbolic of the rainbow of human potential for passionate caring and giving within all of us.

Helping people he didn't know at their greatest time of need, Roberto Clemente died as a volunteer.

Can there be any other higher tribute?

To you, Roberto, a true "Global Force of One," on the 25th anniversary of your magnanimous and selfless action, I dedicate this book of common sense ways to help our fellow man, fellow woman and every child to better our communities, our schools, our environment and ourselves.

John T. Boal
December 31, 1997
Burbank, CA

$1 From Every Book
To Keep Roberto's Dream Alive

Long before he gave his life, Roberto's dream was that youth could be better served by a combination of sports, education *and* community service.

In September, 1993, Roberto's oldest son, Roberto Clemente, Jr., established The Roberto Clemente Foundation (**800 Vineal St., Pittsburgh, PA 15212 ... 412-231-5688**) to extend his father's dream for at-risk youth in Pittsburgh.

A dollar from the sale of every copy of *Be A Global Force Of One! ... In Your Hometown* will be donated to the Foundation as a way to keep Roberto's meaningful message for youth and his powerful compassion for humanity alive for today and the 21st Century.

CONTENTS

PART I
Community

CHAPTER 1: Creative Crime Prevention/Intervention

CHAPTER 2: Portable Programs For Entrenched Problems

CHAPTER 3: **Make Youth Part Of The Process**

CHAPTER 4: **Mainstreaming**

CHAPTER 5: **Raising Standards & Morale**

PART II
Business

CHAPTER 6:   Do What You Do Best For The Communities
You Serve ...

CHAPTER 7: **Portable Ideas For Small To Large Businesses**

PART   III
Schools K-12

CHAPTER 8: Pre-School

CHAPTER 9: Innovative Learning

CHAPTER 10: **Raising Standards, Morale & Resources**

CHAPTER 11: Diffusing/Controlling Behavior

CHAPTER 12: Connecting Into Community

PART IV
Individual

CHAPTER 13: From Me To We

CHAPTER 14: **Digging In For Earth & Wildlife**

CHAPTER 15: **20-Point Front-End Alignment**

INTRODUCTION

We are at a defining moment in history.

As we approach this momentous marker that has only occurred once before in modern history — from 999 to 1000 — the United States is and will continue to be the most powerful and most affluent nation on the planet in the 21st Century.

But at what expense?

Many people today are searching within themselves and asking, "Can't we do better? Can't we find ways to rebuild our lost sense of community; restore our schools and put satisfaction and meaning back into our lives?"

It's a collective gnawing passion ...

To re-gain our capacity for spirited cooperation;

To preserve the precious trilogy of balance among humans, wildlife and the environment;

To re-set the compass in communities to steer the underserved and the physically or mentally disadvantaged into more of the mainstream;

To lessen our neurotic fixation on the shallow elements of our celebrity and sports-driven culture;

To strengthen our infrastructure within the police/intervention/probation/rehabilitation cycle;

To elevate the stature of public school teachers, social service workers and 93 million volunteers helping 570,000 nonprofits;

To empower everyday citizens with the synergy of caring and sharing toward creating a society that provides satisfying and enduring meaning to individuals while creating compelling changes throughout our communities and;

To revitalize our K-12 educational system with an internal dynamism fueled by a genuine curiosity and lust for learning that extinguishes boredom and disengagement so education is no longer society's forgotten stepchild but is at the forefront of technological change complemented by a resurgence of making core subjects ingrained as survival skills and enhanced by a greater emphasis on historical perspective, humanistic values and critical thinking that can collectively create a new intellectual confidence to guide students through all the challenges and stages of life.

"Across the country, one finds a huge, growing hunger among Americans to find more meaning in life — through spirituality, service or both," wrote David Gergen, editor at large, in *U.S. News & World Report.*

Author and Nebraska psychologist Mary Pipher hears the same clarion call ringing from one community to the next. "Everywhere I go, I hear,

'What can I do to help?" she reported in *USA WEEKEND*. "I can tell they are hungry to get organized and get to work. I think they will."

Perhaps a succinct overview from The Trends Research Institute in Rhinebeck, NY summarized it best. "People are looking for direction," said director Gerald Celente. "They're lost."

Air-Raid Warnings

Despite our nation's unquestioned multiple strengths, over the last 20 years we have also received air-raid warnings that we refuse to hear and subsequently ignore without taking long-lasting corrective action.

- First, it was the "A Nation At Risk" report in the early 1980s that foresaw "a rising tide of mediocrity" as College Board scores, literacy and training in science and math were so poor that collectively they would affect the quality of our culture.

Unfortunately, that unheeded report was a near bullseye. According to a November 1997 study of 4500 members of the National Association of Manufacturers, *60%* confessed their current employees lack basic math skills and *55%* have serious deficiencies in basic writing and comprehension skills. That's 2700 individual manufacturing companies saying its *current* employees lack basic math skills and 2475 companies saying its employees have difficulty with basic reading and writing! Is anyone listening?

- Also in early 1982, UCLA professor James Q. Wilson first coined the "Broken Window" syndrome as a telling metaphor for the atrophy of community caring within a society that's based primarily on solipsism. He believes that many communities have succumbed via a broken window ripple effect: If a window remains unrepaired in a building, then it will only be a matter of time before that window gains a perverse sense of legitimacy and makes it acceptable for street kids to break all the other windows. That's what happens when no one in a community cares about taking responsibility outside of their own residence.

- Then in 1995, Harvard University professor Robert Putnam published an article titled "Bowling Alone" that traced the demise of civic and fraternal organizations from Kiwanis to the local bowling leagues.

Each of these warnings, respectively, depicted a slide in our schools, a slide in our communities and a slide in the quality of our individual lives.

Concomitant to these debilitating trends, in the last decades of the 20th Century, we have also witnessed the most damaging race riot in U.S. history in Los Angeles; the most destructive act of terrorism on U.S. soil in Oklahoma City and the most depressing acts of the futility of life with the Jonestown and Heaven's Gate cult suicides.

Something is deeply wrong when there is so much potential literally at our fingertips and yet we recoil initially and then retrench with each new horrifying act and become more desensitized and isolated in the process.

There is no root culprit but we must look closely and honestly at the leadership of every business and every organization and ultimately what drives our culture.

Time For Balance In Business

Money drives just about everything. And that pursuit has created Big Auto, Big Banks, Big Insurance, Big Law, Big Managed Care, Big Media, Big Oil, Big Software and Big Sports among many others that all lead to Big Arrogance, Big Ego, Big Greed and Big Politics.

With these comes an all-too-pervasive-mine-is-bigger-than-yours-oneupsmanship-and-ethics-be-damned-if-we-can-get-away-with-it-militaristic strategic planning that crushes the human spirit by creating organizational mules who are constantly looking over their shoulders for the next downsizing.

With the lightning pace of technological change affecting every big institution externally and the destructive forces of greed and power driving them internally, the critical mass of employees at these organizations disseminates these cold realities to the vendors who support them as well as to family, friends and neighbors. And so it percolates — from the top down — throughout the nation.

"You want to know how leadership works?" asked management consultant Dr. Steven Berglas in *Inc.* magazine.

"Throw out the mission statements; don't bother with values statements; just look at how the company leader behaves and you'll know with 100% certainty how the employees will act and feel about their employer and their employment status.

"If your employees know you to be corrupt, their attitude toward work will be shaped by what you do, your mission or values statement be damned.

When people at the top of an institution behave in a self-centered, narcissistic way; their 'screw the rules' attitude is likely to be emulated by all they come in contact with."

As the cartoon strip "Dilbert" often reflects, rank-and-file employees tend to walk around with cynical theories on how the world operates. They figure, 'Since my company is becoming colder and tougher, I'm going to be colder and tougher to my outside world (witness the rise of Road Rage) and I'll just take care of myself.'

With this widespread cormorant theory settling inside our heads, who then has the inclination to get involved and get committed to our communities and schools and restore the quality of our lives?

In the end, the greed factor grows — and although subtle and never openly discussed — almost becomes like a gene that is passed on to new employees. Eventually it will backfire.

Renowned management expert and prolific author Peter Drucker — who has an uncanny ability to take threads of structural trends and weave them into concise connections — foresees a bubbling backlash against management executives and CEOs with their multimillion dollar salaries. "In the next economic downturn there will be an outbreak of bitterness and contempt for the supercorporate chieftains who pay themselves millions," he predicted in *Forbes*.

But for now — *for the most part* — there is a smug indifference to the outside communities and schools as leaders continue to ignore or refuse to acknowlege the consequences of their actions.

The late Harold Geneen, former head of ITT, best exemplified this isolationist leadership philosophy.

"My theory is that the best community relations in the world, and the clearest expression of social responsibility, is to provide strong, well-paying jobs," he flatly stated in his book, *The Synergy Myth and Other Ailments of Business Today.*

Liquidate Lust-For-Money Before It Destroys Us

True change — major, ethical change of latitude that reins in the excessive lust for more money, more objects, more stock options and more power — must be addressed or this obsessive drive could destroy us.

When our schools go without a basic air conditioning unit and students lug around textbooks printed in the 1970s, how can "leaders" conscientiously buy their 4th car and 3rd home?

Isn't it ironic that although most Americans live from paycheck-to-paycheck, that individuals are responsible for 87% of the $150 billion in annual charitable giving and corporations can only chip in 5%?

Yet, in June 1997, after the owners of the Los Angeles Kings announced their drive to bring an NFL team to Los Angeles, they received checks totaling *$450,000 in the first 24 hours* from local businesses as deposits for luxury suites, according to the *Los Angeles Times.* Are these the same companies whose employees lack basic math and writing skills?

There is also an estimated *$65 to $85 billion* of "corporate welfare" programs that flows *annually* from the federal budget to corporations for projects to aid their basic research or to enhance their foreign advertising budgets.

And while the New Economy is providing a whole new generation of New Wealth, Family Foundations are in vogue for their well-designed tax shrouds. Although some money from these New Wealth Family Foundations has to be distributed, oftentimes it goes to self-indulgent institutions. In addition, according to *U.S. News & World Report*, 8 out of 10 Americans who earn at least $1 million a year leave nothing to charity in their wills.

How long can this crescendo of cynical hypocrisy toward our communities and the myriad of webbed services struggling to connect and protect all of our citizens — in addition to the decades of neglect toward our public education system —continue?

"A cynic knows the price of everything but the value of nothing."
— Oscar Wilde

The value of our communities, our schools and ultimately our individual lives will plummet if business leaders do not begin to balance their corporate responsibilities by universally giving back to the communities that sustain them and by helping to upgrade our schools to raise our nation's stock in the long-term future of the 3rd Millennium.

Yet, despite the prevailing wind, there is a new direction, a breath of fresh air forming and circulating.

"Millennial Fever" — Work Through It

Author and lecturer Jim Rosenfield has studied behavior at the turn of every century from the 1290s on and has identified symptoms of what he labels "Millennial Fever."

"Centuries turn rarely but millennia stagger the sense of time completely," Rosenfield analyzed in *Adweek*. From his research, he's found that people approaching the 21st Century feel "destabilized and in need of reassurance."

Unsettling, yes. But somewhat optimistic, too.

The nation's social framework at the turn of the 19th to the 20th Century was both disintegrating and reconstructing, according to Harvard professor Robert Putnam who is also more hopeful than his "Bowling Alone" theory.

"Get in a time machine and go back with me a hundred years to 1896," he urged in the *Dallas Morning News*.

"What's happening in America? The answer is exactly the same thing. At the end of the century we had a period of 30 to 40 years of dramatic technological change that rendered obsolete a whole stock of social capital. And American society at that time showed all the symptoms of a social capital deficiency; great problems in the cities, concern about political corruption and growing disputes between the classes.

"Then within the first two decades of the 20th Century, American civil society righted itself in one of the country's greatest bursts of innovation. Virtually all of the major civic institutions were created — the PTA, the YMCA, the Boy Scouts, the League of Women Voters, NAACP, the Urban League and on and on. Virtually all were invented in response to earlier forms of social connectedness. And I think we are poised to do a similar kind of thing now."

If we open our hearts and minds and shed our biases and refrain from our ingrained snap rejection behavior patterns, then the global community of mutual giving and caring in all of its unselfish unity will be before us and we can, perhaps, fully embrace the next "great burst of innovation."

Or as other visionaries have so eloquently articulated:

"If you have a chance to do something for somebody and do not make the most of it, you are wasting your time on earth."
— Roberto Clemente

"Everyone can be great because everyone can serve."
— Martin L. King, Jr.

"We must be the change we wish to see in the world."
— Ghandi

"We must always change, renew, rejuvenate ourselves; otherwise we harden."

— Goethe

"If you look closely you will see that almost anything that really matters to us, anything that embodies our deepest commitment to the way human life should be lived and cared for depends on some form — more often, many forms — of volunteerism."

— Margaret Mead and Rhoda Metraux
Aspects of the Present

"The old spirit is still there — buried, perhaps, but waiting for a wake-up call to lift us out of our sourness and self-doubt. We have it in us to create communities committed to deeply held values, shared purposes, economic vitality, self-renewal, and the release of human possibilities; communities that have mastered within their own boundaries the secret of wholeness, incorporating diversity and helping others accommodate it as well ... We have tremendous resources of strength and spirit — but we need to strike a spark to release that spirit."

— John W. Gardner

"Let's crack the atom of civic power."

— Harris Wofford

"The answer lies in the only thing we haven't tried: a massive, nationwide commitment of talented, compassionate, and creative people in our society, a commitment not only to support worthwhile programs and projects financially, but rather to deploy skills and special talents on behalf of people in need, personally. The effort must be focused, sophisticated, organized, and directed toward the toughest tasks, rather than the tasks that are simply the most suitable for untrained but well-meaning volunteers. Just as we can't buy our way out of poverty, we can't volunteer our way out, either. Communities will be transformed only when the people in and around them are transformed. Electoral revolutions will be ephemeral and in the long term irrelevant, unless the next American revolution is a revolution of the heart, a revolution within each and every one of us."

— Bill Shore
Revolution of the Heart

Millennial Showdown ...
Battle For Your Eyeballs & Derrieres

The key to transforming our communities — as Bill Shore so masterfully articulated — is by transforming the people in and around them. We can do that by restructuring our leisure time.

But in our instant gratification society, the battle line will intensify over who holds the attention span of the American consumer during that precious leisure time in the near and long-term future.

Since World War II, we have drifted into a predominantly counterfeit culture where the critical mass of the population increasingly takes the path of least resistance to find new ways to pleasure itself.

Knowing the consumer behaves this way, a Disney executive gave an uncharacteristically frank statement on how this master marketing machine positions itself in this battle.

"Our main goal is to get people to spend their disposable income with properties associated with the company, whether they're our theme parks, videos, movies, or our sports themes," said Tony Tavares, president of Disney's Anaheim Sports, in *Fortune*. "If you've got a dollar, we want it."

Disney is no by means alone in its open aggressiveness for the consumer buck and consumer attention. TV, CDs, commerical websites, movies, concerts, travel packages, amusement parks, ballparks, arenas, speedways and stadiums ad infinitum all beckon ever more persuasively and hungrily for our eyeballs and derrieres.

But what if just 10% of the population shifted from a passive, spectator society that refuses to wait for the next sit-com or the next movie opening or the next parade and instead only watches 3 hours of TV a night instead of 7; sees only 3 movies a month instead of 5; attends only 2 concerts a year instead of 4; goes to only 3 sports events a year instead of 7 and redirects that extra leisure time into a spontaneous passion in the trenches of our communities, local environments and local schools and becomes part of a much more proactive segment of society that develops real life dramas of satisfying personal interaction and, along the way, discovers the SAM Factor?

brace The "SAM" Factor

that defies a convenient "media hook" has been forming, the last decade.

erleader types, this movement is down-to-earth and practical and is on the bubble of that burst of innovation Professor Putnam observed at the beginning of the 20th Century.

Even beyond the 202 entries profiled in this book, there are dozens of other innovative, compelling, human, common sense and portable projects, partnerships, models and new ideas that have created dramatic and verifiable community solutions and school reform that are lighting the torch of civic and self-renewal.

However on her speaking tour, Mary Pipher, author of *Reviving Ophelia,* warned, "Nobody's connecting the dots. Nobody's realizing that these great programs in Ohio are like these programs in Oregon. Grass roots projects all over the country are not being integrated. Because of that, every community has to reinvent the wheel."

Just as our bodies get "jet lag," there is unfortunately a great "adoption lag" of the spreading of these programs that could have enormous exponential impact if they were fully developed and franchised into 1000s of communities. Like yours.

Hopefully this book will help "connect the dots;" considerably shorten that adoption lag; accelerate the replication process and, at the very least, inspire an open-mindedness to rethink how much more productive we can be in our leisure time.

In the meantime, these emerging programs and innovative alternatives are collectively setting a new agenda and redesigning a new personal guidance system for a more sensible, balanced and responsible society. But it can't be a piecemeal response, one program in Ohio, one in Oregon and so on. It must be a wholesale response. It can't be a passive response; it must be a massive response.

On the pages that follow are scores of projects, some of which are national in scope while others are "niche" programs. Yet all are ripe for replication. Each one has an overview summary and most have call-to-action details on how to begin duplicating these programs and partnerships in your hometown or school district. But they need your participation and commitment to expand their goals and missions that, in turn, will begin to create a new heads up era of "conspicuous caring."

This will mean changing habits by becoming less of a spectator and less a part of the conspicuous consumption crowd. As many people have found, those habits are often very hollow pursuits anyway. Yet there's room for all three: spectator, consumer and being a global force of one.

By aligning with these groups, people also find something that's often missing in life and that's the "SAM" Factor:

Satisfaction
Appreciation
Meaning

As we reflect on the significance of the beginning of the 3rd Millennium — and the level of man's evolution — where do more violent-psychotic-moronic-fireball-cliched-end-of-the-world-desensitizing special effects movies; more pathetic "shame is fame" confessional rehabilitation TV; more broadcasts of the Worldwide Wrestling Federation and more saturation coverage of twisted courtroom trials fit into a culture that is hungering for something more satisfying and meaningful and where their contributions will be truly appreciated?

The SAM Factor — receiving Satisfaction, Appreciation *and* Meaning in one experience — seldom comes from work; sitting as a spectator; submitting to electronic manipulation and, unfortunately, less frequently from family and friends but almost always from being a volunteer or activist.

Think about it. There is only one Super Bowl winner, one World Series winner, one NBA champion and one Stanley Cup winner every year. That means over 60 cities have millions of fans burning up millions of hours week after week, month after month.

Are we that desperate for feeling like a winner that we have to live vicariously through overpaid professional athletes who are often laughing behind our backs as they cash their $75,000-a-week paychecks?

Yet nearly every time people volunteer, they're winners.

And it's not just for people with time on their hands.

While the American Institute of Philanthropy estimates there are some 93 million volunteers donating $209 billion annually in volunteer services, this nimble movement is ever so steadily shedding its stodgy image and becoming hipper. From 1991 to 1995, the rate of volunteerism among teenagers, ages 13-17, rose by 7%, according to the Independent Sector.

"I've often thought about how my life would have been so drastically different if I hadn't started volunteering at such a young age," reflected Tara Church, 20, from the office of her award-winning, nonprofit group Tree Musketeers in El Segundo, CA, after 12 consecutive years of volunteer work.

"I would have done the normal things and been fine with them. That's what society expects of a young person. But along the way, I felt a sense of power by volunteering. I felt like what I was doing was very important; that I wasn't wasting my life. I'm out there doing something, making a difference and actually creating a better future for the world. I really feel like I've already gotten so much more out of life than most people get in a lifetime."

Her young legacy of volunteering also paid off in the form of a 4-year scholarship to USC as well as a $10,000 award for community leadership from the DO Something organization among many others.

"A volunteer is priceless, like gold," compared Church. "When a person gives of himself or herself in their spare time, it's like giving money and you should always treat them that way."

Be A Global Force Of One! ...
In Your Hometown

Re-stitching a better quality of life into the fabric of communities, schools K-12 and our personal lives, this book is filled with sustained bursts of innovations and neat programs that are steadily improving the way we live and teach our children.

This is not a trite movement to "take back our communities" or "take back our schools." Nor are these nice pat-on-the-head pet projects of community do-gooders. These are proven ways to *creatively enhance* our existing structures and personal rhythms with fresh, human, compelling and common sense ideas that are readily adaptable.

Based on 2-1/2 years of research, it's a collection of 202 creative and practical programs, projects and partnerships that, if replicated on a widescale, will significantly help address the "Nation At Risk," "Broken Window" and "Bowling Alone" syndromes and help bring satisfaction, appreciation and meaning into our lives, a chunk at a time.

But if you're looking for the "silver bullet," then put this book down now. Unfortunately our society has become so conditioned to "getting it" in a 30-minute or 60-minute TV show, a 2-hour movie or being seduced by such pitches as acquiring "Thinner Thighs in 30 Days!" There is no quick fix or 1-minute marketing mentality to restore our communities and schools or put quality in our lives. It can be excruciatingly tedious and cumbersome in our remote control, electronic society.

Consumer Choice Volunteerism

As consumers, we have become spoiled in the marketplace. We have 100s of customized cars and computer systems, 1000s of mutual funds, 1000s of grocery products, 1000s of clothing options, multiple telcos and now even a choice of utility companies. Perhaps nowhere is this more apparent than when we dine in a restaurant and ponder forwards and backwards on all the entrees, combinations and specials.

To motivate the critical mass which is so accustomed to consumer choice, we can't expect to simply soften people up with warm and fuzzy public service TV commercials and see this great rush of enthusiasm to volunteer.

The critical mass can't be coerced. The motivation has to be cultivated and generated — from the top down, from the citizens up, from the inside out and with considerable multiple choice.

While we want to give back and get involved with our communities and schools, we also want the full menu of volunteer and proactive options so we can link our personal interests with local needs. We simply don't want to be told to volunteer at a certain school at 3 p.m.

This book is that starting menu. For example in the first section on Community there are 57 programs from around the nation that are divided into these 5 chapters:

- 14 programs on "Creative Crime Prevention/Intervention"
- 15 programs on "Portable Programs For Entrenched Problems"
- 7 programs on "Make Youth Part Of The Process"
- 6 programs on "Mainstreaming"
- 15 programs on "Raising Standards & Morale"

Dust Or Dedication?

While many of us approach positive change with initial enthusiasm, a lot of us often drop off along the way without that gritty stick-to-it-tiveness to make things happen and create permanent change. Or we listen to that collective chorus of resignation that chimes, "That's the way it is ..."

Yet the 1000s of people behind these programs refused to listen to that popular chant ... refused to accept the conventional pyschobabble of cynics ... refused to play victim ... and refused to take no but instead took responsibility and created changes for the better and, a la Ghandi, they themselves became the change they wanted to see in the world.

So instead of collecting dust on a shelf, hopefully this book will inspire you or someone you know into action.

Specifically, it's divided into 4 parts:

- Community
- Business
- Schools K-12
- Individual

When seemlessly soldered together, these are the foundations to support a continuously improving and value-added culture for current and future generations. Ideally, more than a few of the 202 entries within these 4 parts will specifically trigger your personal hot button or the button of a member within your circle of family, friends and co-workers. For example:

- **In the Community section** ... You know a city councilman who wants to expand your town's recycling program. You could get him information on starting a new "Community Composting Facility."

- **In the Business section** ... You may notice the "Volunteer Accountants" which is of no interest to you but may be just right for your Uncle Bob in Durham, NC who's a community-minded spirit who happens to be an accountant as well.

- **In the Schools K-12 section** ... Your son has an art aptitude but his school's program is weak. You could contact "ARTS Partners" in Houston to begin replicating that exemplary school art program in your son's school.

- **In the Individual section** ... Your dog-loving neighbor might be interested in contacting "Canine Companions For Independence." Under this group's guidance, your neighbor could raise a Corgi puppy for 15 months after which the puppy goes back to the organization. It then would train the dog more and later turn it over to a disabled person to help them with their independence.

To dedicate yourself to the *Be A Global Force Of One!* process, think in terms of how you can link these worthy groups, nonprofits, partnerships, projects and ideas to people in your address book, neighborhood, gated community, condominium or apartment building as well as school friends, co-workers, fellow executives or casual acquaintances from the Post Office, grocery store or even your "Cheers" bar. In other words, think outside of your personal box and spread these around as a new daily habit.

Also, try not to think in terms of just touching base with 1, 2 or 3 programs. To truly bring these groups into the mainstream of society, think in terms of contacting dozens, either by phone, mail or visiting their websites. Then embrace these programs as an ongoing, all out effort to reconstruct your weekday and weekend leisure time into more enjoyable and satisfying experiences that can easily be incorporated into your lifestyle on a year-round basis and not just during the soft holiday season between November and December.

Make it a 12-month commitment to change not only the course of your life but also the course of our culture.

Cross-promote Community & Education Renewal?

As a small first step to compete with mass marketers of leisure and entertainment which only want you to hand over your brains and your wallet at the door, nearly 100 logos were included to help give these programs consumer-oriented images in a concerted effort to show how progressive nonprofits and community partnerships have become as they slowly gain a foothold in the mind share of the American public.

In addition, a minority of American businesses — from NYSE corporations to consultants to Main Street enterprises — *have* picked up the baton of putting something back into their communities and schools by doing what they do best or by initiating innovative projects. A few of these include Southwest Airlines' "Home For the Holidays," Mervyn's "ChildSpree" and Pfizer's "Sharing the Care" among 29 such projects in the Business section. Their logos were included as well. *(In all usage of the logos, not one nonprofit or company paid for the exposure.)*

Although many other companies and industry associations *have* committed to primarily mentoring and tutoring programs vis-a-vis Colin Powell's "America's Promise — The Alliance For Youth" campaign **(703-684-4500 or http://www.americaspromise.org)**, the large and small companies in this book were selected to represent as wide of a crossection of industries as possible and to stimulate other companies in these and related industries to devise similar programs where there is a return-of-services-or-products into communities or schools. *Yet no profitable business has an excuse not to do more* for their school districts and hometowns from where it pulls its revenues. Denial, detachment and isolated operating practices are not acceptable anymore.

"Business in the 1990s cannot operate as a unit separate from the rest of society," stated John Castle, board member of The Points of Light Foundation and an executive vice president at EDS. "To be effective, we must connect all parts of the community into a cohesive unit."

Providing jobs and paying taxes are just baseline. While writing a big check to a foundation is noble, it's over and done with when the check is signed off. Also, sometimes a generous gesture is only a veil to the ongoing merchandising of an image or for something worse. "In general, the more noise made about the donor's largeness of heart, the more likely he is engaged in self-promotion or outright bribery," wrote Michael Lewis in *The New York Times Magazine.*

Also needed are time, human commitment, energy, ideas, enthusiasm and the sharing of struggles and triumphs which are priceless, just as appreciated and often more meaningful.

Dramatic change in our society cannot occur without the business world getting more involved, both financially and with services, technology and manpower. But it doesn't have to be an overkill solution as most business leadership approaches problems.

It could be something as simple as creating a "Scholarship Circle" for students within a 5-mile radius of an office. Or it could mean becoming an active member of the Business Coalition for Education Reform. Or it could mean helping communities, schools and environmental groups think, promote and publicize in modern marketing terms. For example, a company could assign its marketing department, ad agency, public relations firm or graphic designers to create an identifiable "brand" or image beyond a logo; design their website; help them cross-promote or share resources with other groups to enhance each other's credibility or begin a "Cause-Related Marketing" campaign which ties a social issue or cause to the merchandising of a company's products or services.

The latter is especially intriguing as the first-ever research in this area — the 1997 Cone/Roper Cause-Related Marketing Trends Report — found that *76% of consumers would be likely to switch* to a brand associated with a good cause if price and quality are equal. **For more information, contact Cone Communications, Inc., 90 Canal St., Boston, MA 02114 or call 617-227-2111.**

========

The next 10-15 years have the potential to be a most fulfilling, enriching, exciting and dynamic period. We ARE at a defining moment in history. Preventions, cures and technological breakthroughs are coming at us with unprecedented speed.

Yet — admist the technical advances — we must jumpstart individual, social, community, educational and environmental progress as well to keep up with the beat. If we don't upgrade our schools; reduce our greed; safeguard our citizens; diffuse our personal animosities; provide more equity for minorities; protect our environment and endangered species; move from a sense of "Me to We;" erase the cool indifference of youth and make our communities livable, safe and sustainable, then at some point it will only take a gust of wind to blow this house of cards down.

But with the 202 entries on the following pages, we have an *initial* national menu, a *beginning* roadmap, to harness the human spirit and imagination; to pave a new road of uncommon alliances such as teenagers becoming Young Adult Police Commissioners; disabled people gaining self-esteem on horseback; low-income neighborhoods banding together against landlords in Small Claims Court; Tibetan monks teaching patience to gangbangers and retired doctors giving free health care to the working poor among scores of new circles of cooperation among nonprofits, for profit companies, industry and trade associations, communities, schools and individuals which are all blending and working together; to fuel and expand these emerging infrastructures and to redirect our focus on solutions needed today and for the 21st Century.

If each one of us first sheds our initial skeptical tendencies and embraces the firm belief that a single individual *can* make a difference — and then goes out and contributes in some way to improve our individual habitat and the community, schools and environment around us — then each one of us can *Be A Global Force Of One!*

PART I

Community

Here are 57 innovative community projects, programs and ideas with contacts for replication in your hometown.

They were selected for their:

- Creativity;

- General ease of adaptability throughout the U.S.;

- Potential long-term impact on the quality of the entire community;

- Ability to be initiated by a single citizen with a phone, pen or Internet access;

- Ability to deter crime with demonstrable results; give disenfranchised children a better chance of having normal childhoods; empower youth earlier than traditional expectations; enhance the care and treatment of domestic violence victims; assist older adults; help homeless populations; improve or solve local environmental issues; equalize the financial responsibility of child-raising; address racism; foster safety; mainstream disabled people; upgrade local technology access and generally inspire communities to pull together by lifting their collective spirit and developing a new and meaningful vision for the 21st Century.

CHAPTER 1

Creative Crime Prevention/Intervention

Community

COMMUNITY #1

"Nite Lite"
Boston's Police & Probation Partnership Triggers Nation's Biggest Drop In Major Crime

Sickened by seeing 16 juveniles on probation murdered between 1988 and 1989, Boston probation officer Bill Stewart was making idle but very frustrated conversation outside a courtroom one day.

'Let me ride in a patrol car at night so I can pull probation violators who are out past their curfews off the streets instantly,' Stewart essentially blurted to Det. Robert Fratalia who agreed with his spontaneous suggestion, according to *The New York Times*.

Initiated in 1992, "Nite Lite" has since become lights out for youth ages 17-25 who are on probation in Boston.

Some of the spectacular results include:

- Juvenile homicides dropped 80% from 1990 to 1996
- Juvenile assault and battery arrest rate dropped 65% from 1993 to 1995
- Court-ordered compliance of probation has risen from 15% to 70%

While also reducing inter-agency egos; creating tighter communications; significantly increasing mutual respect and building trust for sharing crucial criminal information, the program elevates Probation Officers from little more than 9-5, courthouse check-in monitors to on-the-street, in-the-home *strict enforcers* who are ready to re-arrest without probable cause, without a search warrant, without a new trial and without a free get-out-of-jail card.

Other programs in the comprehensive Boston Police package include:

- **Boston Gun Project**   Targets supply side of guns using a computer linked to data run by the Bureau of Alcohol, Tobacco and Firearms in Washington, DC.

- **Operation Cease Fire**   A zero tolerance policy against violence in 4 gang neighborhoods.

- **Youth Violence Strike Force**   45 police officers and 15 state and federal agency officers working together.

Together these programs dropped the number of Boston homicides in 1996 to 59, a remarkable 30-year low.

For more information on this complete prevention, intervention and enforcement strategy, contact Commander, Youth Violence Strike Force, 364 Warren St., Roxbury, MA 02119 or call 617-343-4444.

"Shortstop"
Short Circuits First-Time Offenders With 92% Success Rate

Although serious adult crimes have dropped in recent years, juvenile crime is on the rise. And according to criminologists, it could get worse as there is a boomlet of young violent males coming up in the population.

Thus jolting first-time offenders to stay straight is a critical turning point not only in their lives but also for their families and communities.

One program in particular called "Shortstop" *has scored an astounding 92% deterrent rate with English-speaking offenders and a 78% deterrent rate with Spanish-speaking offenders* one year after graduation, according to the *Los Angeles Times*. This covers 16,000 offenders and their families who completed the sessions.

Founded in 1980 by the Orange County Bar Foundation, Shortstop is a rugged attitude alignment for kids ages 10-17.

Maiden criminals *and* their parents are put into a mock lock-up where wards from the California Youth Authority present "reality therapy" of their simulated future life in the criminal system. Each kid is also provided a souvenir "mug shot" as a permanent reminder and gets the privilege of sitting in the "Hot Seat" where he or she is grilled by attorneys about their crime and its ripple effects.

Even worse (for some) is the mandatory completion of 10 writing assignments including separate parent and child eulogies as if the offender had died.

With Shortstop's high success rate, a widespread implementation of this program would seemingly help stem the tide against what likely will be a growing plague on our nation.

For more information, contact Shortstop, P.O. Box 18498, Irvine, CA 92623 or call 714-851-2570, ext. 148.

"Safe Streets Now!"
Forecloses On Drug Houses By Taking Landlords Into Small Claims Court

Taking the fear out of neighborhoods from terrorizing local drug cartels; returning safety to the night and mobilizing neighbors in our all-too-isolated society may seen like a daunting and insurmountable challenge.

But the award-winning, Oakland, CA-based Safe Streets Now! has created a powerful community-action package that leverages the legal system to put the clamps on gutless and greedy landlords who are so callous to residents living as hostages either (inside) or near drug or crack houses, prostitution hotels or slacker liquor stores.

In one of Safe Streets Now's more high profile success stories, the California Supreme Court allowed a contested $218,325 judgment to stand in favor of 75 Berkeley residents over 2 landlords who failed to curtail the drug activities in a 36-unit apartment complex.

This easily-adaptable framework for lassoing in landlords has 4 basic parts:

* Community Action Guide
* 12 Customized Story Boards
* 2-day Training Seminar
* Step-by-step Trainer's Guide

The package outlines how "to document the public nuisance" of a drug house and its demoralizing effects on a neighborhood; how to conduct the legal and property research on a landlord and how to file and collect a class action suit in Small Claims Court.

While most of the Safe Streets Now! programs have been implemented in California, it can be blended to communities in any state. And while there is a $7000+ fee for the training and materials, Safe Streets Now! is a bargain considering its high success rate; the multiple dividends of a crime-free neighborhood; a cash settlement to citizens and a return to a better quality of life.

With an average turnaround time of just a few months from training to your collective day in court, Safe Streets Now! is definitely worth a call.

For more information, contact Safe Streets Now!, 408 13th St., Ste. 452, Oakland, CA 94612 or call 800-404-9100.

"MAD DADS"
Conducts Neighborhood "Street Patrols" During Gang "Street Hours"

A courageous community mobilization, MAD DADS is comprised of committed fathers who walk and talk right into the dens of their most violent neighbors.

For example, in the Crenshaw district of Los Angeles, a team of black, green and white uniformed MAD DADS first outlines 10 city blocks and then patrols the area from 9 p.m. to 1 a.m. on Friday and Saturday nights. Over a dozen young men have been directly impacted by this strolling band of surrogate fathers.

Formed in Omaha, NE in 1989, MAD DADS — Men Against  Destruction - Defending Against Drugs and Social Disorder — has been adopted by 52 communities in 14 states. (Crime in communities where residents work together on the problem can decrease as much as 40%, according to a comprehensive survey in the journal *Science*.)

NOT a vigilante group, MAD DADS is a multi-ethnic, sustained intervention, non-intimidating group that conscientiously challenges the violent tendencies of its local youth with constructive conversation and positive alternatives to their terminally destructive lifestyles.

Collectively, MAD DADS has made contact with over 700,000 wayward youth. For many of them, it was their first moment-of-truth with a concerned adult male role model during their teenage years.

For more information on this high impact community program, contact MAD DADS National Headquarters, 3030 Sprague St., Omaha, NE 68111; call 402-451-3500 or visit their website at http:// www.maddadsnational.com.

COMMUNITY #5

"TARGET"
Hits Bullseye
With 41% Drop In Gang Violence

Incensed by a string of 3 gang murders of innocent teenagers over a 6-month period in 1992, 60 community leaders in Paramount, CA — from the City, School District, Sheriff's Department, District Attorney's office, Probation Department, churches, businesses and private citizens — banded together to form TARGET, Team Approach Regarding Gang Enforcement Techniques in 1993.

Arguably the most aggressive anti-gang organized response in California, TARGET pinpoints 25 of the most violent gang members based on criteria in the Street Terrorist Act. These 25 are then told they will be contacted as many as *4 times a day* to document their hour-by-hour activities.

Other parts of the TARGET program include:

- Alternatives to Gang Membership
- Bike Patrol
- Gun-Sniffing Dog
- "Owl" Patrol Cars (at banks and convenience stores)
- 72-hour Response to Graffiti Removal

Funded by a 2% Utility User Tax providing $1 million a year for the program, TARGET dropped gang-related violent crimes by 41% in the first year.

For more information on this powerful gang reduction program, contact TARGET, City of Paramount, 16400 Colorado Ave., Paramount, CA 90723 or call 562-220-2155.

"ONE CHURCH - ONE OFFENDER"
Breaks Cycle Of Recidivism
From 50% To 16%

Maiden criminals, who have only crossed the line once, are getting re-aligned with an innovative program called ONE CHURCH - ONE OFFENDER, the only U.S. program that combines churches with criminals in a structured way outside the penal system.

Initiated by Rev. Clyde Adams in Fort Wayne, IN, these criminal adoptions have dropped recidivism to 16% of the cases in this program whereas the Allen County Jail in Fort Wayne has a 50% recidivism rate.

Here's how it works:

First-time offenders who did not use a weapon; who served their sentence or who are under parole are assigned to a group of 5 trained volunteers from a sponsoring church. They pool their knowledge and community resources and focus their energies on a single client. The group serves as a surrogate family providing encouragement to help the offender finish his or her education or get a job.

Since its inception, over $600,000 has been saved annually by the community. Also, 46 churches with over 200 volunteers are now involved in the ONE CHURCH - ONE OFFENDER program.

Make it happen in your hometown too. It only takes a single citizen to make that call.

For more information, contact ONE CHURCH - ONE OFFENDER, Inc., 227 East Washington Blvd., Ste. 205, Ft. Wayne, IN 46802 or call 219-422-8688.

"ONE CHURCH - ONE ADDICT"
Uses Team Approach
To Snap Drug Habits

Drug addicts — from marijuana to heroin — who've made mental contracts with themselves to finally stop their habits often face unexpected battles to recovery.

Too frequently they encounter lack of family support; expensive medical programs; bureaucratic bungling at treatment centers; well-intentioned but jaded therapists and job insecurities. The confusing jambalaya of insensitivity can often lead right back to the addiction.

A new form of intervention, with some parts divine, weaves a caring "team ministry" of 4-6 members (one of whom is usually a recovering addict) into a blanket of social, practical and confidential support topped with "tough love" focused on working tirelessly with a single addict at a time, knowing that relapses are inevitable but loss of will is unacceptable.

Formed in 1994 by Rev. George Clements, ONE CHURCH - ONE ADDICT has been implemented by over 700 faith communities with over 400 addicts in various stages of recovery.

While treatment professionals are quick to dismiss this recovery plan, ONE CHURCH - ONE ADDICT is not only cost effective as the team's expenses run only about $360 per month but it also creates a renewal of purpose for any religion — regardless if it's Christianity, Judaism, Muslim, Buddhism, New Age or Scientology — to reach within its members to pull together for those who desperately need help in their communities.

With the theme "Love the addict, hate the addiction," ONE CHURCH - ONE ADDICT makes uncommon sense for widespread implementation to achieve self-renewal for addicts committed to kick their habit into permanent remission.

For more information about this model program, contact ONE CHURCH - ONE ADDICT, 1101 14th St., NW, Ste. 630, Washington, DC 20005 or call 202-789-4333.

"TRIAD"
Tosses Safety Net Over Older Adults

Often targeted as easy prey, older adults or their loved ones can be a part of a creative crime prevention approach called TRIAD that is now in place in more than 500 counties.

Here's how it works:

The county sheriff, local police chiefs and representatives of a local senior organization (such as AARP) get together and devise focused prevention programs that enhance the response and delivery of police services as well as reduce unwarranted fear within that particular community.

Each county establishes a Seniors and Lawmen Together (S.A.L.T.) council to run their customized crime prevention campaign.

Here are some examples:

- Cruising on golf carts hooked with radios connected to the police department, volunteer drivers take shifts watching for suspicious activity in shopping center parking lots in Ruston, LA and Medina, OH.

- Uniformed officers drop in periodically at the homes of more than 500 older adults in Western Massachusetts.

- In a program called Carrier Link in Clark County, WA and elsewhere, postal carriers contact the local police department if more than a day's mail accumulates at an older adult's residence.

For information about starting TRIAD in your hometown, contact TRIAD, 1450 Duke St., Alexandria, VA 22314 or call 703-836-7827.

"Community Police Academy"
Expands Role Citizens Play In Law Enforcement

Taking citizen involvement up several notches from simply calling the local WE TIP hotline by educating the community in multiple police tactics such as the proper use of force is an innovative citizen's course implemented by the Los Angeles Police Department.

The 9-week Community Police Academy course provides an excellent primer for cultivating synergy between the local police and the community it serves.

Sample topics include:

- Crime Scene Investigations
- Drug Enforcement
- Firearm Training
- Internal Affairs and Discipline
- Jail Tour
- Patrol Procedures
- Vice Activities

There is no fee and all participants receive a certificate of completion at the graduation ceremony.

Initiated in 1995, the Academy is an enlightening way to strengthen the lines of communication and the bonds of mutual understanding between citizens and police departments.

For more information, contact Community Police Academy, Los Angeles Police Department, 251 East 6th St., Los Angeles, CA 90012 or call 213-485-6586.

Slam a Headlock
On Domestic Violence

Approximately 70% of all female homicides are committed by abusive husbands or boyfriends according to *The Journal of Trauma*. Domestic violence is every community's problem.

While solutions aren't simple, more and more communities are finding ways to make a concerted attack on this disgusting syndrome that, in the past, was often swept up under the community blotter.

For example:

- Nashville, TN has cut its domestic murders *in half* by **fast tracking legal and criminal procedures** including setting bail as high as $100,000; having detectives thoroughly investigate all complaints and insisting on tight coordination among police, prosecutors and judges.

- New York City now has **special courts to handle** *only* **domestic violence cases**.

- Washington, DC has **a team of judges overseeing all aspects of domestic violence cases** instead of having separate judges handling different issues.

- The Los Angeles Police Department has equipped **400 patrol units with high-end Polaroid cameras to document violence** on the spot. Great idea, but troublesome execution as the Department has had some difficulties keeping film in stock.

- Judge Richard Denner of Los Angeles Superior Court has **trained 130 advocates from women's shelters and low-income law centers to file restraining orders by fax**. Within 24 hours, a Family Law Judge will reply by fax and hand down the orders. Faxes are also sent to the LAPD and Sheriff's Department.

- The Los Angeles County District Attorney's Office has established a 2-person Stalking and Threat Assessment Team to **track convicted stalkers after they complete their jail terms**.

- In the San Fernando Valley in Southern California, there are Domestic Violence Clinics that use **"Volunteer Advocate Coordinators" — especially bilingual volunteers — to help women cope and break free from their violent relationships**.

- Apartment Movers of Lincoln (NE) provides **free moving services to women trapped in violent residences**.

- The Denver-based ADT Security Services has given **15 electronic security pendants to women under constant siege** in each of over 124 communities across the U.S.

With effective *changes* now taking place, it only makes sense to rapidly deploy these tactics in every community to begin eradicating this despicable violent crime.

6 Afterschool Programs To Combat "Prime Time For Crime"

According to the Pacific Center for Violence Prevention in San Francisco ...

- Younger children, ages 6-11, are more likely to be crime victims *at 3 p.m.* than at any other time.
- Youth, ages 12-17, are more likely to be crime victims during the hours of 3 p.m. to 11 p.m.

More than ever, communities need to rethink and rebuild their afterschool programs for youth. Here are 6 programs among many good ones to consider:

BOYS & GIRLS CLUBS OF AMERICA   Although the Boys & Girls Clubs of America began at the same time as the Civil War, its most dramatic growth has occurred since 1987 with the addition of more than 1000 new Club locations. Its enrichment, development, health and sports programs are unmatched for afterschool activities for youth ages 6-18. With a revitalized presence and extensive relationship marketing with national companies, a Boys & Girls Club should be a natural for every community. **For more information, call 404-815-5700.**

CLUB DENVER   Denver's 19 middle schools have 6 different afterschool "clubs" open from 2:30 p.m. to 6 p.m. The themes relate to city functions and extend the school-to-career instruction students receive in class. The clubs include Arts, Aviation, Firefighters, Medics, 21st Century Teachers and Platte River (conservation and restoration project). **For more information, call 303-640-3250.**

KENNEL KIDS   Natural bonding agents — kids ranging from ages 6-18 and homeless animals at an animal shelter — get together everyday after school. What a clever connection. Since 1994 at the West Haven (CN) Animal Shelter, over 200 children have been "Kennel Kids." The children feed the animals; clean their cages; walk the dogs and develop responsibilities toward their favorites who look for them everyday. This antidote to afterschool apathy could easily be started in any community. **For more information, call 203-937-3642.**

L.A.'s BEST   "Cool" afterschool fishing trips in the Long Beach Harbor, computer training, Space Camps, dance competitions and homework assistance are just a few of the engaging programs offered by this award-winning, model enrichment program for 5000 inner-city kids ages 5-12 at 24 Los Angeles elementary schools. With waiting lists at most sites, L.A.'s BEST has attracted interest from more than 180 cities. Operating from the end of the school day to 6 p.m., 245 days a year and energized by committed volunteers and a staff working out of the Mayor's Office, the unique program is a partnership of the Community Redevelopment Agency, the Los Angeles Unified School District and corporate sponsors. **For more information, call 213-847-3681.**

LIGHTED SCHOOLS   Using community resources such as arts organizations and medical institutions, 4 Waco, TX middle schools have opened their doors after the normal school day ends by offering arts, cultural and recreational activities. What's most impressive is this program came out of a coalition of 83 public and private organizations all working together. **For more information, call 254-753-6002.**

WORKING CLASSROOM   A sophisticated afterschool art, drama and writing program in neighborhoods surrounding downtown Albuquerque, NM, this highly-honored nonprofit organization is a national model for unleashing and nourishing the inherent talents of youth in "historically ignored communities." Hard-hitting bilingual plays, public murals, publishing and classroom storytellers are just a few of its artistic avenues for creative expression. **For more information, call 505-242-9267.**

Tibetan Monks Make Gang Members Contemplate Sounds Of Nonviolence

Combine the most "negative" male group with the most "positive" male group in our global community and what do you get?

The karma of inner-city enlightenment!

Just imagine ... 6 Tibetan monks ... spending 30 days at a probation camp of hardened Southern California gang members ... imparting their nonviolent ways through chanting ... and then tapping out grains of brightly-colored sand into a "mandala," a 3-foot granular painting, and later symbolically scattering it into the Pacific Ocean.

To say this is a "community outreach" program would be the understatement of the century.

Nevertheless it happened in late 1995 at Camp David Gonzales, a probation camp in Calabasas, CA.

Initiated to spread Tibetan culture to the West, this creative coupling called "Healing The Causes of Violence" was the brainchild of Barry Bryant, director of the New York-based Samaya Foundation.

Although a month of monks is not nearly enough time to reverse a life of criminal behavior, there were enough signs to say that their peaceful lifestyle did have an impact and made some re-alignments along the way.

Photographer Ricardo DeAratanha. Copyright 1995, Los Angeles Times. Reprinted by permission.

While most kids came out of the Tibetan classes with a much calmer attitude, one 18-year-old carjacker did admit in the *Los Angeles Times*, "When I came here, I didn't have no patience. When somebody looked at me wrong, I'd hit them. Now I got patience." Another 16-year-old confessed he's now found a way to break his cycle of failure.

"These small healings that take place each day, those are the important ones," Bryant emphasized. "They're little baby steps, and this is where we can crack the violence and experience nonviolence. This will start them on the road to self-esteem, and the essence of this program is self-esteem. It is not about religion. We teach the fundamentals of being healthy and being a part of a healthy community."

What if, what if this highly improbable but inspirational program were adopted and expanded to probation camps, juvenile halls and prisons throughout the U.S?

Not only would the goal of the Foundation be reached but so would the core of this country's criminal element. Just imagine!

For more information about initiating "Healing The Causes of Violence" in your community, contact the Samaya Foundation, 75 Leonard St., New York, NY 10013 or call 212-219-2908.

Faux "LAPD Video Zone" Banners Help Deter Street Crime

Turning to the "David Copperfield era of law enforcement," the Los Angeles Police Department in cooperation with local businesses and apartment owners raised more than a few eyebrows when it hoisted a string of 20 red-and-white street banners on one light pole after another with ominous messages flapping in the wind: "Buy Drugs, Go To Jail" and "LAPD Video Zone."

Purchased by members of the community in the Parthenia Street neighborhood of suburban Northridge, the block long repetition of strong warnings creates a unique and riveting reinforcement to the dire consequences.

Sure, it may only be an illusion to the residents of the large, low-income apartment complexes who live near the banners, but to drug dealers coming into the area for the first time, it can be the only deterrent they need to leave as they quickly see a united community front to root out drugs ... the crucible of most major crime.

Photo by Delmar Watson

Cool Community Combo:
Police & Rec Center Under One Roof

One of the most disarming ways that police are gaining the upper hand in tough neighborhoods is by implementing foot and bike patrols.

Citizen-friendly, community policing is a powerful weapon against crime. Now here's another way to enhance it.

Through a public, private and philanthropic partnership, the Los Angeles Police Department has entrenched itself deeper into dozens of communities by building Community Service and Youth Activity Centers.

One such 12,000 sq.ft. center in suburban Reseda not only houses a bike patrol but also a positive arsenal of activities for kids. These include pinball games, pingpong tables, a boxing ring, foosball tables, an outdoor basketball court, weight & exercise equipment, a computer and homework lab.

By creating a recreational/educational magnet for local youth and having the police nearby in a non-threatening office, positive and permanent community relations are fostered by repeated visits in an inviting atmosphere.

For more information, contact the LAPD Community Service and Youth Activity Center, 19040 Vanowen St., Reseda, CA 91335 or call 818-756-8406.

CHAPTER 2

Portable Programs For Entrenched Problems

Community

COMMUNITY #15

"SANE"
Tulsa's 30-Minute RN Response To Rape Victims Is a Sane Solution For Every Community

One out of 8 ... 12.5% of U.S. women.

Approximately the same percentage of women who get breast cancer is also the percentage of women who will be raped, according to the Justice Department.

Yet despite suffering through the trauma of the violent act itself, women typically suffer again in the aftermath:

- Humiliating 3-5 hour wait in Emergency Rooms
- Often insensitive and incomplete forensic exams

- No fresh clothes or shower
- No counseling
- Ultimate indignity of being billed $600 for treatment

In the heartland of America, a superior and sensitive program has put some common sense and compassion into this ongoing, tragic black mark on our society.

Called the Sexual Assault Nurse Examiner program, SANE is a rapid response, community-based approach that, in only 30 minutes, mobilizes a medical crime collection and victim rehabilitation team which has an impressive 88% conviction rate of rapists brought to court.

After a police officer calms the victim and collects the basic information, he or she calls the dispatcher who calls the Crisis Hotline which has a monthly schedule of 16 beeper-connected RNs who are trained in forensic exams of rape victims.

Within half an hour, the RN arrives at a specially-equipped suite at one of Tulsa's 5 hospitals where the nurse begins a15-step forensic exam which usually takes 2.5 hours. In addition, a Volunteer Advocate arrives to start psychological counseling. And the Oklahoma Crime Victim Compensation Board pays a $100 fee to the nurse for her services and $50 to the hospital. The victim, does not, and should never pay for anything.

Since 1991, the SANE program has conducted over 1360 exams. Of the 34 cases that eventually went to trial where the on-duty RN testified, there were 30 convictions!

Besides winning the prestigious Innovations for State and Local Government Award in 1994, SANE's nurse examiner concept has been replicated in approximately 125 communities. But every town should immediately adopt this incredibly SANE approach ... in 30 minutes or less!

For more information, contact SANE, Tulsa Police Department, 600 Civic Center, Tulsa, OK 74103 or call 918-596-7608.

"Trench Projects" Help Drain Racism From Pores Of Society

Racism should, but won't, be erased in the 21st Century. It's an intolerable hand-me-down from one generation to the next.

Legislation, court decisions, TV insult shows, bumper stickers, commissions, town hall dialogues, T-shirts, songs and stilted Presidential kaffee klatsches have generally been ineffective, not from intention, but from measurable result. Unfortunately, they're mostly exchanges of opinion that don't *change* behavior.

Shared actions do.

When a common experience such as military service or sweat equity is shared, attitudes start changing. The experience of suffering together or working together greatly bleaches the bias and becomes a common denominator for mutual understanding and acceptance.

For example:

• After a year-long series on race relations in the *Akron Beacon-Journal*, 200 community groups formed the innovative "Coming Together Project." It has sponsored such projects as a Walk/Run for Unity and a Picnic/Baseball Game as well as hosting twice a year workshops in the schools among other ways that are fostering local racial harmony. **For more information, call 330-379-3830 or visit their website at http://www.ohio.com/comingtogether.**

• In the tiny community of Bluefield, WV, citizens used the symbolism of improving a bridge that links the black community with the white community. Over 65 volunteers put aside their differences and picked up paint brushes to upgrade the largest structure that brings them together.

• In Nashua, NH, the New Fellowship Baptist Church received help from the established (white) Grace Lutheran Church to refurbish the Baptist Church's new facility. All races worked together in harmony.

- In Baltimore's Sandtown neighborhood, a black-and-white partnership formed through the New Song Community Church has made great strides to mutual trust by building a school and a medical center together.

What symbolic structure separates one race from the other in your hometown? Is there a way to refurbish that structure to begin uniting the differences? Are there other community facilities that are needed and used by both races? Or in time of disaster, could your all-white or all-black group offer helping hands to a burned out rec center or church?

Community "Trench Projects" are not just single-shot gestures either. A bronze marker could be placed on the building, bridge or facility signifying when it was completed and who was involved in the project.

This way the symbolism could be passed through the generations until one day, hopefully, racism just fades away.

"Government Access" TV
Puts The Heat On Deadbeat Parents

Not just for family, friends and gadflies anymore, "Government Access" TV programming is putting the heat on deadbeat parents in Charlotte, NC.

Since 1995, the city's Government Access channel has been airing 10-12 capsule summaries of deadbeat parents along with 10-12 snapshots of Mecklenburg County's "Most Wanted" local criminals on the run.

During the first few months it aired, millions of dollars in arrears were collected as deadbeats were quickly turning themselves in or co-workers did it for them. **For more information, call 704-336-2395.**

========

Marriages may not last as long as they once did but responsibility for children lasts forever. In California — where only 14% of the state's 3.5 million children of divorce gets the amount they deserve — the Los Angeles County District Attorney's Office opened a website in June, 1996 to track down "L.A.'s Most Wanted: Delinquent Parents" who are failing to pay child support. Its home page is at **http://www.co.la.ca.us/da/childsupport** and is also being used to help locate abducted children.

In addition, the California Department of Social Services distributes a large "Most Wanted" poster of deadbeat parents which has a nearly 50% apprehension rate over 4 years.

Cable listings, posters and websites can all help improve your community by using the synergy of media to turn up the heat on slacker parents.

"HERO"
Reduces Homelessness With 70% Success Rate

HERO is not a sandwich anymore.

HERO is **H**omeless **E**mpowerment **R**elationship **O**rganization.

It is a well-balanced program that fulfills the hunger to be completely independent. And it works 7 out of 10 times.

What started out as a friendly debate between comedian Louie Anderson and his pal buddy, Susan Hassan, has evolved into a model program eliminating pockets of homelessness, one person at a time.

Very simply, the HERO program works so well because it matches homeless individuals *willing* to make and stick to goals with community volunteers who are passionately committed to helping them achieve those goals leading to independence.

The HERO program has a 70% success rate with 140 out of 200 individuals who are living independently, free of drugs and alcohol, and are either working or attending school.

For more information, contact HERO, 3800 Packard Rd., Ann Arbor, MI 48108 or call 313-669-8128.

How To Discourage Homeless Habits And Create Step-by-Step Re-entry Programs

The omnipresent clusters of drifting homeless people are a persistent problem in most communities. And most homeless are forced to become public nuisances as they panhandle at ATMs and intersections for subsistence.

While many communities have homeless shelters, others have devised creative ways to redirect aimless handouts into basic existence and empowering programs to help the homeless re-enter society. Here are a few of these programs:

- **Ban on Aggressive Panhandling**   Santa Monica, CA has passed an ordinance that makes it tough on street people who use hardball tactics for a handout. It's a very effective deterrent as the police issue mostly warning citations instead of actual tickets.

- **Homeless Donation Program**   Two money collection sites in a high profile section of Santa Monica called The Promenade brought in $35,000 for social programs. This program deflected the need to give to panhandlers as citizens are assured their money is going directly for constructive uses and not to the nearest liquor store.

- **Clean-up Waystation**   Another Santa Monica program is its innovative SHWASHLOCK, an acronym for SHowers, WASHers and LOCKers. This is a public facility where homeless people can get themselves and their clothes cleaned. This turnaround center has done just that as it has helped many people become *ex*-homeless people.

- **Voice Mail Boxes**   Community Voice Mail started in 1991 in Seattle. This free voice mail system helped 125 out of 145 homeless people find jobs in the pilot program. To offer this basic communications link for the homeless in your community, **call 206-441-7872.**

- **Help Cards**   Pocket-sized cards listing dozens of help numbers such as AA, Clinics, Shelters and Referrals are handed out to the homeless in Studio City, CA.

- **Help the Homeless Vote** Help turn out the "homeless vote" in your community by contacting the National Coalition For the Homeless (NCH) and asking for its "You Don't Need a Home To Vote" packet that tells exactly how communities can start uplifting the homeless by getting them to the voting booth. **Call 202-775-1322 for the NCH packet.**

- **Homeless Art** Since bottled-up homeless people have few outlets for expression, the Homeless Advocates of San Diego coordinated 13 working artists to start art classes for homeless people. That initiative led to 2 art exhibits and a renewed sense of confidence for these neglected voices.

While some may perceive the ban on panhandling to be punitive and others may view the rest of the programs to be mere band-aids that don't address the underlying issues of our nagging homeless population, these very basic step-by-step programs do rectify immediate needs in low cost and creative ways and can become turning points in people's lives.

"Family Pathfinders"
A Model Texas Program Leads Families Out Of Welfare & Into The Community

Since the 1996 federal welfare reform law was enacted, the nation's welfare population has dropped to a 28-year low. Despite its "success," welfare recipients still need a bridge to lead them back into the mainstream.

The state of Texas has created a holistic approach that enlists civic clubs, congregations and corporations to individually shepherd a motivated welfare family back into the community for a period of 12 months.

"These groups have a unique ability to supplement state aid with the kind of one-on-one, personalized help no government can provide," explained John Sharp, comptroller of public accounts for the state of Texas.

"It complements the work these organizations already do by helping them target specific families on public assistance and focus on their immediate needs. And it underscores the fact that a sound family structure is at the heart of real welfare reform."

Initiated in 1996, "Family Pathfinders" is completely voluntary and confidential for these emerging families.

Some of the needs addressed include:

- Arranging child care
- Coaching for job interviews
- Organizing finances
- Training for computer skills
- Tutoring ...
- But no financial aid

For more information on adapting this program in your community, contact Family Pathfinders, Comptroller of Accounts, P.O. Box 13528, Austin, TX 78711; call 800-355-PATH or 512-463-4000 or visit their website at http://www.window.state.tx.us.

"SOS Children's Villages-USA"
Builds a Family Anchor For Foster Children

Every community has an abundance of foster children aimlessly bouncing around the system.

Every community also knows it could and should do more to restore some semblance of family to the growing numbers of abandoned, abused, neglected and orphaned children.

Now motivated communities can link into the nearly 50 years of experience of building foster villages worldwide with the relatively new SOS Children's Villages-USA.

Established in 125 countries, SOS started the tedious process of building foster villages in the U.S. in 1992 and today has sites in Coconut Creek, FL and Lockport, IL with others under construction in Milwaukee, WI and Washington, DC.

There are 4 principles to every SOS Children's Village:

- **Caring Parent**   A screened and trained parent makes a long-term commitment to raise a family of children.

- **Connecting Brothers & Sisters**   An emphasis is made to re-unite biological siblings who were separated in the foster care system.

- **Hearth & Home**   Each child lives in a permanent home where the rituals of childhood such as meals, homework, birthdays, holidays and memories are shared and enjoyed.

- **The Village Cluster**   A group of 8-15 such homes and a community center comprise the Village Cluster which is designed to blend in with the surrounding community where the children can then attend local schools, churches and social activities.

Communities must be deeply committed to pull the levers to build these foster villages. Creating a local board; generating private support and enlisting the involvement of public officials are the essential ingredients to develop and sustain this truly visionary community village.

To begin, contact SOS Children's Villages-USA, 1010 Pendleton St., Alexandria, VA 22314 or call 800-886-5767.

"Free Arts For Abused Children"
Cries Out For Nationwide Adoption

Innocently trapped in the shadows of society, abused and abandoned children will needlessly suffer a litany of emotional traumas as adults. During that time, they will spend years of agony trying to resolve their troubled childhoods.

However, creative expression during those high pressure, bottled-up days can siphon some of their festering despair and act as a balm to the youthful soul.

Since 1977, one nonprofit group in particular has been successfully enabling young people to vent through the arts.

Free Arts For Abused Children is a nonprofit West Los Angeles group that directly impacts 3500 children each month through 400 volunteers who help deflect their day-to-day disarray through drawing, dance, music, painting and sculpture.

"I've seen the faces of so many children light up with Free Arts' volunteers," reflected Dr. Barbara Firestone in the *Los Angeles Times.* "They give the children a vehicle to express their feelings, activities to participate in that are non-judgmental. That experience is a precious gift to children who have been abused, abandoned or neglected and it promotes their healing."

Running a range of programs, volunteers go directly to the public facility where the victimized children are placed. There they customize projects to each child. A 20-week commitment permits the children to get comfortable with the caring volunteers so they can acclimate to loosening up and begin the healing process.

A nationwide adoption of this exemplary community effort could make a lasting difference in the lives of so many neglected children.

For more information, contact Free Arts For Abused Children, 11965 Venice Blvd., Ste. 402, Los Angeles, CA 90066 or call 310-313-4278.

"Community Technology Centers"
Hook Up Your Hometown

Although there is little debate on the absolute link between computers and most careers — both today and into millennium — how do you plug in equitable computer access to the 60% of U.S. households which do not have PCs to make it as accessible as borrowing a book at the library?

Fortunately, there is a national "parallel port" that connects into communities with the resource contacts and step-by-step functional framework to deliver technology to the socially and economically disadvantaged in every community to ideally teach people multi-task computer skills that can lead to successful careers.

 A leading advocate of public access to computer education, the Community Technology Centers' Network (CTCNet) has over 250 affiliates which have established fully-equipped centers in Boys and Girls Clubs, YMCAs, Housing Authorities and Commissions, Public Libraries and other local venues throughout the U.S.

With its detailed "Center Start-Up Manual" covering Mapping Community Assets, Staffing, Software Selection, Space and Hardware, Scheduling, Budgeting and Preparing a Business Plan, CTCNet also offers other publications, affiliate conferences, hardware/software donations and partnership programs as well as many resources and tips on how to establish an easy access computer education center in your community.

To hook up your hometown, contact the Community Technology Centers' Network, 55 Chapel St., Newton, MA 02158; call 617-969-7100 or visit their website at http://www.ctcnet.org.

COMMUNITY #24

Assuage Every Mother's Guilt And Lessen The Load On Landfills With "Community Composting"

How many times have you seen a normally sane Mom tear herself to pieces over her children and neighbor children not eating everything on their plates? Or maybe you are that Mom!

'Do you know how many starving kids in Africa have nothing to eat today?' she asks the universal, rhetorical question to blank stares.

Well, motivated Mothers who want to siphon off as much as 70% of everyday waste to beneficial use rather than disposal may want to get together and form a coalition to bring composting to their community and to their backyards.

There are now over 3000 composting facilities in the U.S. processing millions of tons of organic material. Besides a frequently missing component in the community recycling loop, composting improves soil fertility; provides erosion control; restores wetlands; purifies land through bioremediation and makes Moms less guilt-ridden.

Since 1990, The Composting Council has been stirring implementation of individual and community composting programs. Their resource-rich library includes dozens of publications. To start a hometown composting campaign they have:

- Community Issues in Facility Siting
- Compost Facility Operating Guide
- Compost Facility Planning Guide
- Compost Facility RFQ/RFP Development Guide
- Compost Information Kit
- Compost Marketing: Planning Guide for Local Governments
- Compost Workshops

A clearinghouse and a catalyst, the Council is not only linked to other organizations but also has many more programs. One of the more innovative projects, called "Food for the Earth," initiates composting in the huge, untapped restaurant and foodservice industry.

For more information, contact The Composting Council, 114 S. Pitt St., Alexandria, VA 22314 or call 703-739-2401.

"Environmental Sustainability Kit"
Creates a Long-Term Community Vision

Making a new, more livable community vision a democratic process is not an easy task.

But a neighborhood in Portland, OR simplified the procedure by having local residents take walks with architects who drew sketches on-the-spot so participants could immediately see their particular vision spring to life.

This is just one of the sound ideas spread throughout the  "Environmental Sustainability Kit" prepared by the Environmental Defense Fund. This solid and sensible kit focuses on the environmental and pollution prevention aspects of making communities sustainable and integrates creative strategies and tools to supplement the primary theme.

One of the easily adaptable ideas in the Case Studies section is a "Good Neighbor" Agreement between a community and a local business or industry that contains "provisions covering pollution prevention and implementation specifics." Fortified by federal right-to-know data on the chemicals companies are using, this agreement acts as a benign first strike initiative to let businesses know pollution prevention is a major line of defense to sustain a community.

Cost of the kit is a bargain at $15. For more information, contact the Environmental Defense Fund, 1875 Connecticut Ave., NW, Ste. 1016, Washington, DC 20009; call 800-684-3322 or visit their website at http//www.edf.org.

"Community Support Project"
When Environmental Encroachment Hits Home, Here's Who To Call ...

With the relentless push for development, community friction frequently erupts when a commercial enterprise becomes a hazardous or destructive encroachment on citizens who are ill-equipped to defend their turf.

 People who are frustrated with not having a voice of reason with local politicians or their Community Redevelopment Agency should consider the "Community Support Project" at the Friends of the Earth with offices in Washington, DC and Seattle.

Helping individual citizens, neighborhood groups or grass roots environmentalists, the Community Support Project specializes in water and waste arenas with a growing expertise in clean air issues.

Staff at the Project can:

• Perform targeted environmental research for a quick response to a local issue.
• Simplify the understanding and enforcement of environmental regulations.
• Provide "issue papers" on municipal landfills, U.S. water quality standards and environmental impacts of oil, steel and manufacturing plants.
• Groom local activists with an overall environmental finesse to make high-powered opponents less formidable.

They have helped groups oppose an expanded gravel quarry; prevent dioxin emissions from a paper mill; ban backyard barrel burning; stop dirty fuel emissions from a power utility and the building of cellular phone towers among dozens of other environmental encroachments infringing on the quality of life. (They cannot provide financial or "on-site" assistance.)

For more information, contact Community Support Project, Friends of the Earth, 1025 Vermont Ave., NW, Third Floor, Washington, DC 20005; call 202-783-7400 or visit their website at http://www.foe.org/

"Trust For Public Land"
A Savvy Lifeline To Help Hometown Parks & Green Spaces Survive & Thrive

As communities continue to experience steady declines in federal and state conservation funding ...

As community leaders are often lobbied to sell valuable city property to sharp developers who are keenly aware of exigent city budget demands ...

As 16 out of 23 inner-city communities in the U.S. have inadequate or overcrowded parklands ...

A steely oasis of sanity and sophisticated financial intervention to protect, preserve and expand parks and green spaces is available at The Trust For Public Land (TPL).

 With over 25 years' experience, this nimble nonprofit — with 26 nationwide offices — can quickly mobilize professional real estate, legal, mediation and financial consultants to help communities get "bridge financing" to hold a piece of property until public funds are available. Then TPL sells the land to public agencies at or below fair market value. In 1996, TPL helped over 100 communities protect 69,000 public acres.

By positioning parks and green spaces as prevention assets that have statistically proven to reduce crime as well as raise property values and the overall quality of life, TPL has launched a "Green Cities Initiative" to guide cities to purchase 100s of parcels for future city parks.

However regardless of where your community is located, TPL can provide technical assistance for purchasing land in any of these public areas:

- Bike & Mountain Trails
- Community Gardens
- Greenways
- Inner-city Parks
- Recreational Areas
- Restoring Historic Sites
- River Corridors
- Suburban Parks
- Waterfronts
- Watersheds

For more information on all of their land preservation programs, contact The Trust For Public Land, 116 New Montgomery, Ste. 400, San Francisco, CA 94105 or call 800-714-LAND.

"Renew America"
The Mother Lode Of Solutions To Benefit Mother Nature

Communities struggling with knotty environmental issues should — before putting them on the agenda at City Council one more time — consider pawing through the 1500 successful local solutions that have been carefully screened and archived at Renew America (RA).

Since 1989, RA "has been the only national organization specializing in identifying, verifying and promoting model programs that protect, restore and enhance the environment."

In its 150-page *Environmental Success Index*, 1500 model programs are listed in 26 categories from Atmosphere & Climate to Community Education to Forests

& Rangelands to Freshwater & Watersheds among others. Each one has a capsule summary detailing the program with contact information for replication. (This database is also online at RA's website.)

Some of RA's 1996 award-winning programs include:

- Blufflands Alliance
- Buffalo Restoration Program
- Don't Do It In The Lake (anti-dumping campaign)
- Latex Paint Exchange
- ReThink Paper
- The Green Classroom
- Volunteers Reforesting America

To order a copy of the Index ($25) or receive more information, contact Renew America, 1400 Sixteenth St., Ste. 710, Washington, DC 20036; call 800-922-RENEW or visit their website at http:// www.crest.org/renew_america.

Rebuild Communities
"From The Inside Out"
Mobilize The Mundane Miracles
Of Existing Assets

Turning traditional community redevelopment completely upside down are 2 men from Northwestern University who have creatively mapped a way for low-income communities to build from the inside out.

"The key to neighborhood regeneration is to locate all of the available local assets, to begin connecting them with one another in ways that multiply their power and effectiveness, and to begin harnessing those local institutions that are not yet available for local development purposes," wrote John Kretzmann and John McKnight at the Institute for Policy Research at Northwestern University in the introduction to their warmly humane work, *Building Communities From The Inside Out.*

By diagramming a "Community Assets Map" that defines the existing assets i.e., individuals, associations and local institutions, and by replicating 100s of examples across the U.S. that are "internally focused" and "relationship driven," the authors firmly contend that long-lasting community rebirth can begin.

Here's just one example:

- After surviving demolition from city redevelopment, the Pike Place Market in Seattle regenerated itself by offering a medical clinic, child care, a senior center, housing units, a food bank, food coupon program and a home for street youth.

For citizens who are committed to rebuilding from within, this book of specific ideas linking individuals and existing assets is an absolute MUST READ AND HOW TO GUIDE for 21st Century communities.

To order a copy ($15), contact ACTA Publications, 4848 North Clark St., Chicago IL 60640 or call 800-397-2282.

CHAPTER 3

Make Youth Part Of The Process

Community

Let Teens Rule ... For a Day

Making teenagers feel a part of their hometown is a daunting challenge for every community.

Yet one small town has creatively embraced this task by annually handing over the reins of power and responsibility to approximately 20 local high school students for a "Youth in Government Day."

For over 7 years in Santa Clarita, CA, selected students prepare for their political power trips by researching city issues and the positions held by their mentors. Then during their reign, they shadow their mentors throughout the day; present reports and hold their own City Council meeting with gavel-to-gavel recordings of the proceedings.

Community role reversals are an excellent way to promote understanding and appreciation for the grit and grind of getting things done and keeping a town in tow.

In addition, not only can students become surrogate city ambassadors but they may also see a career path they hadn't considered.

"Teen Court"
Puts a Clamp On Crime

With a goal of "educating young people rather than punishing them," Teen Court — where teens impose sentencing on teens committing misdemeanors — is now successfully operating in over 300 communities.

In New Mexico, where there are 22 Teen Courts, this form of peer punishment has had a significant impact. Repeat offenses among juveniles have dropped from 50% to 9% in Albuquerque alone.

Here are the rules of Teen Court:

- Only first-time offenders under 20 years of age
- Only misdemeanor crimes
- Defendants must plead guilty prior to sentencing
- A volunteer lawyer oversees the proceedings
- Defendants must be a juror at some point
- Sentencing, usually 10 to 125 hours of community service, is strictly enforced

For a nationwide list of Teen Courts, contact the American Bar Association/Public Education Division, 541 N. Fairbanks Ct., Chicago, IL 60611 or call 312-988-6386.

"Young Adult Police Commissioners"
With 22 Teens As Advisors,
New Haven Cops Protect, Serve & Listen

Teen Beat has a whole new meaning in New Haven, CN.

A superior national model of intelligent and common sense community cooperation has effectively diffused tensions and embraced mutual respect between 2 traditionally antagonistic groups: Teens and Police.

The "Young Adult Police Commissioners" (YAPC) consists of a racial mix of 22 teens between 13-18 who meet a minimum of once a month and prepare "policy advisories" on all police actions involving teens. Of the 22 commissioners, the Mayor appoints 16 while 6 others are elected from each of New Haven's high schools.

Perhaps the essential key to the success of YAPC stems from an attitude of "adult leaders who are willing to sit down and have serious conversations with young people, without any reservations whatsoever," explained Det. Tom Morrissey, YAPC's original youth coordinator in *CATALYST for Community Crime Prevention.*

This open-mindedness also resonates in the official policy statement that says, "These 22 young people will have the ear of the Department. The Department cannot promise to act on every recommendation they make, but it does promise to give their recommendations on youth topics a fair hearing and to listen to them as it would to adults."

And since 1991, they have indeed listened. Here are some of the recommendations that have been enacted:

- Banned a citywide teen curfew
- Convinced legislators to keep 110 beds in drug treatment centers
- Persuaded the Mayor to buy books in lieu of metal detectors
- Raised money for a children's AIDS hospice

To learn more about this exceptional youth empowerment program, contact Juvenile Services Unit, New Haven Police Dept., 1 Union Ave., New Haven, CT 06519 or call 203-946-6290.

"Youth Congress"
San Diego Activists
Create Revolutionary Model

Revolutions occur in the darnest places.

Among the bursting bougainvillea laced with the pungent scent of suntan lotion lies the youth-obsessed, high activity nexus of San Diego.

This is not your typical feisty environment pushing for dramatic change. Nonetheless, in 1994, over 200 people attended the first "Youth Congress" meeting and established a voice in the decision-making process of firmly-entrenched local institutions that impact their lives.

"Far too often programs are established for the benefit of youth, yet the adult organizers don't get any input from the young people who (sic) they are hoping to help," defined executive director Sophonya Simpson in *Build* magazine. "The Youth Congress stands for a partnership ... a balance of power."

Here's how the Board of Directors is composed:

- Co-chairs (One under 18; one 19-24)
- Secretary (One under 24)
- Treasurer (One under 24)
- Area Representatives (2 representatives from each of San Diego's supervisorial districts; one under 18; one 19-24)
- Special Populations (2 representatives from underserved populations; one under 18; one 19-24)
- Adult Representatives (2 over 25)

One of their success stories was an implementation of basic rights for kids housed in juvenile hall.

For more information on bringing a balance in decision-making for the youth in your hometown, contact San Diego Youth Congress, 4438 Ingraham St., Ste. 2, San Diego, CA 92109 or call 619-490-1670.

Link Into Leadership Labs ...

Future Leaders Are Groomed For Only $350 In Steamboat Springs

Designed "to feed the leadership pipeline," an innovative, 9-month community leadership program of 20 selected residents in their 20s and 30s has helped propel Steamboat Springs, CO to be named as the #2 rated small town in *The 100 Best Small Towns in America.*

✦Leader shipSteamboat

Called "Leadership Steamboat," the program identifies and trains emerging leaders by having them serve on local boards and commissions; making community field trips to major employers;visiting local media and participating in retreats to present reports on community service opportunities as well as offer their evaluations.

"I've gotten a heightened sense that I can have an impact here, that I can make a difference in Steamboat Springs," noted Alan Gildersleeve, a Washington, DC transplant who was one of the first graduates of the program, in *USA WEEKEND.* "That's appealing to me, coming from back East."

Jointly sponsored by the Steamboat Springs Chamber Resort Association and Colorado Mountain College, the program's down payment in the future stock of the community is only $350 payable by the participant, employer or sponsoring organization.

For information on this model community leadership program, contact Leadership Steamboat, c/o Steamboat Springs Chamber Resort Association, P.O. Box 774408, Steamboat Springs, CO 80477 or call 970-870-4455.

========

"DO Something"
Offers $190,000 To Young Leaders Who Are Hip & Helpful

While some youth may sneer at community involvement, others are cleaning up.

In 1996, DO Something — a national nonprofit organization that provides leadership training, guidance and financial resources to young people under 30 who are building their communities — created their first annual BRICK Award for Community Leadership.

The grand prize winner received a grant of $100,000 while 9 others received grants of $10,000 each for a total of $190,000 distributed to 10 young men and women.

For more information on the BRICK awards and all the other dynamic and entertaining ways that DO Something is making it hip to be helpful in the community, contact DO Something, 423 West 55th St., 8th Floor, New York, NY 10019; call 212-523-1175 or visit their website at http://www.dosomething.org.

"Youth on Board"
Pumps New Blood Into Boards Of Directors

Let's be honest. Between you and me and whoever else reads this book, local Boards of Directors are always well-intentioned but are often out of touch.

And in your community are many energetic, sophisticated, street smart teenagers and young adults who are also earnest but often feel out of touch.

Voila! Since many Boards frequently serve youth without a direct, mouth-to-mouth pipeline into their fast-changing ideals and opinions, it makes perfect sense to put them together.

Sadly, up until 1994, the arc between these groups had never been connected. According to a 1994 survey by the Center for Nonprofit Boards, *not one* had any board members under the age of 21.

At the epicenter of this evolutionary change is a visionary group known simply as Youth on Board that easily facilitates the shoehorning of young people onto community Boards of Directors. Formed in 1994, Youth on Board offers a host of programs and services that accelerates youth into active participation on Boards.

Their centerpiece publication is *Youth Governance: 14 Points to Involving Young People Successfully on Boards of Directors*. They also have introductory seminars, the Springboard Training Institute and the Boardblazers Technical Assistance Program among others.

For more information on how to pump up your Board, contact Youth on Board, 58 Day St., Third Floor, Somerville, MA 02144 or call 617-623-9900.

Every Community Should Have This Battle Cry: "I Want My CITY YEAR!"

Out of high school. Out of work. Out of touch.

That's an unwelcome triangle of discontent many frustrated 17 to 23-year-olds face despite their best efforts to become a part of society.

Yet now there is a model community program directed at this age group that can help pave their way into the mainstream.

Known as an "urban Peace Corps," City Year is a 1-year service organization that unites young adults of rainbow backgrounds and various incomes into teams of 10-12 dressed in colorful red, tan and black uniforms to march into their communities and provide grass roots assistance in public schools, housing programs, gardens, food banks and homeless shelters.

This invigorating mix of youth receives a weekly paycheck of $135, health insurance and is eligible for up to $4725 in voucher funds to extend their education or job training.

Initiated in 1988, City Year is a private-public partnership supported by the federal government's Corporation for National Service (which includes 3 AmeriCorps initiatives among others), foundations, corporations, individuals, states and municipalities. For one contributor, it's had a high return on investment.

"City Year is the most cost effective grant in the history of philanthropy at BankBoston," said Ira Jackson, a bank vice president.

Harnessing the energy and idealism of youth at pivotal points in their lives into such a constructive and collaborative service program screams for implementation in many more communities throughout the U.S.

For more information, contact City Year, 285 Columbus Ave., Boston, MA 02116; call 617-927-2500 or visit their website at http://www.city-year.org.

========

For a regional list of the AmeriCorps programs in your area, contact AmeriCorps, 1201 New York Ave., 8th Floor, NW, Washington, DC 20525; call 800-942-2677 or visit their website at http://www.cns.gov.

CHAPTER 4

Mainstreaming

Community

COMMUNITY #37

Hitch Up To a Horse
And Help Someone To Walk!

Nearly every community has horse people and ...

Nearly every community has disabled people.

Hitching these communities together are 100s of groups that practice "Therapeutic Riding" — blending physical therapy with equestrian skills — which has created 100s of miracles on horseback.

"I have seen the wonderful things that the relationship between disabled athletes and horses can bring," passionately described Gloria Hamblin, program director for Ride On in Chatsworth, CA.

"Physical, mental and emotional improvements are all nurtured in the riding arena. Riders with poor balance and lack of muscle tone strive to sit up as the horses' constant movement makes them work harder than they ever would in a clinic — and they love it. Kids with low self-esteem who have only failure find themselves in charge of a huge animal, able to tell it what to do and where to go — something others have been telling them all their lives!"

By defying their disability, almost every type of disabled person can benefit from therapeutic riding.

Throughout the U.S., there are over 500 Therapeutic Riding centers helping over 26,000 individuals with disabilities discover a new found sense of balance, confidence and, in some cases, the ability to walk again.

For more information on how to start a Therapeutic Riding program in California, contact Ride On Therapeutic Horsemanship, 21152 Chatsworth St., Chatsworth, CA 91311 or call 818-700-2971. Outside California, contact the North American Riding For The Handicapped Association, P.O. Box 33150, Denver, CO 80233 or call 800-369-RIDE.

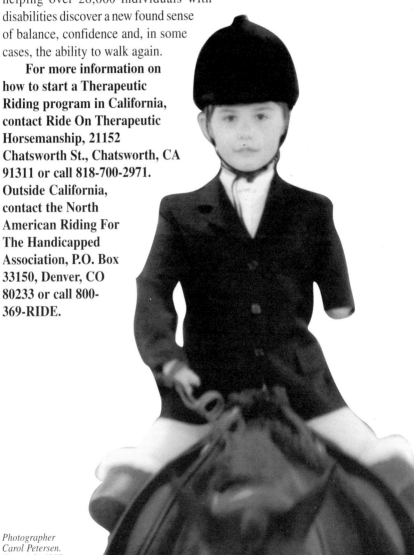

Photographer Carol Petersen. Copyright 1997, Carol Petersen.

COMMUNITY #38

It's "Play Ball!"
For Kids With Disabilities

Does your community have a baseball league for kids with disabilities? If not, consider a "Challenger League."

After all, children with physical and mental disabilities yearn to swing for the fences just like other kids do.

Take one frustrated parent who couldn't find a baseball program for her child, a phone call and you have the Challenger League founded by

Photographer John Beale.

Jeff Bisdee, director of recreational therapy at the Rehabilitation Institute of Pittsburgh in 1991. At the first sign-up, over 90 excited kids registered.

"No one else would help her and I couldn't say no due to my love for baseball!" explained Bisdee who formed a parent volunteer committee to help run the show.

There are no stats and no spats in the Challenger League. Just tons of fun for kids with Down's Syndrome, autism, spinal cord injuries and brittle bone disease.

Each player is joined on the field with a "buddy," giving the field the look of pandemonium with 18-20 people on the diamond. Each buddy helps his or her player bat or field. The infield has 2 sets of bases so there's a set for the player and a set for the buddy. This prevents collisions as players run to their bases on foot or scoot along in a wheelchair.

Every hometown could serve its kids better with a Challenger League. Just announce it and they will come.

For more information, contact The Rehabilitation Institute, 6301 Northumberland St., Pittsburgh, PA 15217; call 412-420-2337 or 412-521-8011, ext. 244.

"Eyecycle"
Tandem Biking Is a Tour de Force For Visually Impaired

Blind people need exercise too.

But unfortunately just about every form of fun exercise requires some hand-eye coordination or a sense of direction to be heads up on where in the heck you're going.

Except on a tandem bicycle where someone else can be the "eyes" of the bike.

EYECYCLE

On the back of the bike you only need a set of piston-pumping legs (and a healthy sense of adventure) to get a good workout.

Integrating such exercise with empathy is the visionary Eyecycle, Inc. founded in 1989 in Santa Monica, CA.

On weekends, sighted volunteers — known as "captains" —are paired with the visually impaired — known as "stokers" — and together they pedal down the Santa Monica Bike Path for a leisurely 14-mile jaunt. The captain also doubles as a tour guide giving a rolling description of the weird and wonderful parade of people who happen along the way.

On a bicycle built-for-2, here's an innovative idea that could easily be adapted and enjoyed by millions of visually impaired people.

For more information, contact the nonprofit Eyecycle, Inc., 720 Wilshire Blvd., Ste. 200, Santa Monica, CA 90401 or call 310-458-2777.

Able The Disabled
With a "Job Fair"

Although there are 49 million Americans with some kind of disability, it doesn't always preclude an ability to draw a paycheck.

Unfortunately, 70% of people with disabilities between 18-65 are unemployed.

What they may lack in physical capabilities, they frequently compensate with their can-do attitude. And many employers have realized the value of retaining reliable, skilled employees is far more important than the peripatetic nature of able-bodied employees.

To show the progressiveness of your community, hold regular Job Fairs for the disabled.

It's a win for the community's reputation for raising the quality of life for the underserved.

It's a win for the disabled who are still experiencing resistance finding solid employment.

It's a win for companies seeking loyal employees.

How can anyone lose? Step right up to that open microphone at your City Council meeting and push for a Job Fair for the disabled until it becomes an event.

"Very Special Arts"
Helps People With Disabilities Become Artistically Empowered

Every community has a commitment to enhance the lives of those citizens with disabilities.

Now they can expand the possibilities by taking advantage of the multiple art education opportunities available through Very Special Arts (VSA). VSA is a nonprofit organization founded in 1974 by Jean Kennedy Smith to create learning opportunities for people with disabilities, especially children and youth.

By immersing in creative writing, dance, drama, music and the visual arts, people with disabilities gain self-confidence; lift their learning skills and improve their overall well-being.

There are 8 "programming initiatives" available through VSA. They include:

- Start with the Arts: 64 learning experiences for children 4-6
- VSA Panasonic Young Soloists Program
- VSA Native American Project
- The Legacy Program
- VA/VSA Program
- VSA Playwright Discovery Program
- VSA Yamagata International Visual Arts Program
- VSA Festivals

Very Special Arts programs are conducted through VSA affiliates and a network of organizations in 50 states and 86 countries worldwide. (Six new programs are in development.)

For more information, contact Very Special Arts, 1300 Connecticut Ave., NW, Ste. 700, Washington, DC 20036; call 800-933-8721 or visit their website at http://www.vsarts.org.

"Wheel To The Sea"
Ripples With Replication
For Other Wheelchair "Hikes"

Even with basic "wheelchair access" fairly common at parks, lakes, trails and other recreational areas, individuals with physical disabilities and their loved ones and friends still have a difficult time experiencing the true "outdoors" as other people do.

One innovative group has significantly lowered the hurdles;expanded the horizons and raised the satisfaction bar by greatly enhancing and even challenging the mobility of people in wheelchairs.

Created by The Wilderness Institute, "Wheel To The Sea" is a naturalist-led (and volunteer-assisted) group "hike" within the Santa Monica Mountains that meanders for 4 miles along a dirt trail; crosses legendary Pacific Coast Highway and rolls down to the beach where the California Park Service provides Sand Chairs which have balloon tires making it easier to push through the sluggish sand.

There the volunteers and participants end the all-day event with a family style barbecue provided by the local Kiwanis Club of Thousand Oaks.

Since many communities are not near an ocean, this ingenious Wheel To The Sea could easily be replicated to any recreational area, e.g. "Wheel To The River ... Lake ... Dam ... Waterfall ... Historical Site, etc."

For more information on this access program, contact The Wilderness Institute, 28310 Roadside Dr., Ste. 140, Agoura Hills, CA 91301 or call 818-991-7327.

CHAPTER 5

Raising Standards & Morale

COMMUNITY #43

"Free Bike Projects" Test Community Spirit & Trustworthiness

Not since the movie "E.T." has a bike-themed project captured the magic and enthusiasm of the public more than the free "Yellow Bike Project" has in Portland, OR.

From a modest gathering of 60 recycled, one-gear, mellow yellow bikes that were introduced at a press conference in September, 1994 in downtown Portland, the program now has over 500 bikes with many still tooling in and around the city, free of charge user-to-user, while others are unfortunately squirreled away in garages.

"Free community bikes promote more efficient transportation; a cleaner environment; assist community policing; burn calories; get unused bikes under needy riders and build hope, trust, sharing, honesty and recycling," explained Tom O'Keefe, founder of Portland's Yellow Bike Project, who has since left the program.

After this free community bike concept wheeled into national attention, over 60 communities adopted similar projects — but with mixed results. A program in Hermosa Beach, CA started with 35 bikes but later few could be found. Yet in the biking bedrock of Boulder, CO, over 100 of its bikes roam free from user-to-user.

To pump new spirit into your hometown — and test the trustworthiness of your citizens — contact Community Cycling Center, 2407 NE Alberta, Portland, OR 97211; call 503-288-8864 or visit their website at http://C2.com/ybp/.

Chattanooga Gets It Right First Time With Vision 2000; Then Sustains Its Renovation With "Re-Vision 2000"

If your community is searching for a roadmap to civic and economic renewal, then contact Chattanooga Venture and book a flight to the nation's premiere turnaround city.

In 1984 — at the city's lowest ebb — a partnership of private, business, city and county leaders came together and suspended all the traditional rules of renewal.

Driven by a mission to tap the mental fiber of everyone, citizens' hopes and dreams were widely solicited; *written down on blackboards;* distilled and then clearly defined into 40 goals.

By 1992, some 8 years later, 37 of the 40 goals had been completed. This tedious but ever so rewarding process directly generated $790 million in new investment throughout the Chattanooga area.

Here are just a few of the accomplishments:

- Auditorium Renovation
- Chattanooga Network Enterprise (low-cost housing)
- Electric Buses
- Family Violence Shelter
- "Made In Chattanooga" Exhibit
- New Cultural Center
- Theatre Renovation
- "Walking Bridge" and Riverwalk

Reinvigorated by their "overnight" success during those 8 years, Chattanooga Venture started all over again by "following a cycle that never returns to the same place."

So in the spring of 1993, a mostly new crop of citizens generated 2559 ideas and boiled them into 27 new goals with 122 recommendations. Called "Re-Vision 2000," they're all clearly defined in a brilliantly designed roadmap aptly titled "A map for our future."

If you're serious about reinventing your community, then run don't walk to your phone and pursue this citizen inclusion model with focused passion.

For more information, contact Dr. James Catanzaro, Chattanooga Venture, 4501 Amnicola Highway, Chattanooga, TN 37406 or call 423-267-8687.

Put Community Dreams On Billboards

Even in the age of the Internet, the behemoth billboard still has its place as a communications tool in communities.

And while most people tolerate their commercial messages, one community created a way to embolden their citizens via billboards by placing the Community Dreams of school children on them instead of Got Milk.

In North Berkshire, MA, children submitted 250 essays and poems on the Martin Luther King "I have a dream" theme. The 7 best were put on billboards donated by Callahan Outdoor Advertising so people could see what the kids in town were dreaming for their futures.

It was so popular that in addition to the outdoor billboards, 50 entries were compiled in a *Book of Community Dreams* that was sold as a fundraiser.

To instill pride, it has to be planted early and then promoted. And the kids and citizens of Northern Berkshire did just that. Dream the possible dream in your community.

For more information, contact Northern Berkshire Community Coalition at NASC, Box 9075, North Adams, MA 02147 or call 413-662-5519.

Photo by Craig Walker/Berkshire Eagle

Resurrect Community Caring With a "Volunteer Fair"

What if you planned a party; expected 300 people to attend and 7000 showed up?

Would you call "911 Catering" or squeeze everybody in?

Community leaders in Springfield, MO did the latter when they held "The Good Community Fair" on January 13, 1996 and 7000 citizens overwhelmed a tiny college student center seeking applications to sign up for such groups as Big Brothers Big Sisters of America and the Interfaith AIDS Network among 118 other community agencies.

Organizations that were expecting to sign up 10 volunteers signed up dozens!

With promotional pushes from 5 radio stations and a 14-part series titled "The Good Community" in the *Springfield News-Leader*, the amazing response tapped into a collective community subconscious that craved to volunteer everywhere.

"We will find ways to get people involved," explained Randy Hammer, executive editor of the *News-Leader*. "If there's any lesson learned, it's that people will make a difference when they know how." Working in concert with the Denver-based Alliance for National Renewal, a similar "Volunteer Fair" was held in 1997 attracting 18,000.

Founded in 1994, the Alliance for National Renewal (ANR) is a program of the National Civic League and is comprised of more than 190 community-spirited alliances, associations, centers, commissions, coalitions, councils, exchanges, foundations, networks, partnerships and services focused on resolving or improving community issues.

ANR is a blockbuster resource of community technical assistance books, guides, handbooks, manuals, conferences, newsletters and a website filled with ideas and ways to fortify neighborhoods and communities.

For more information on their multiple resources, contact the Alliance for National Renewal, National Civic League, 1445 Market St., Ste. 300, Denver, CO 80202; call 800-223-6004 or visit their website at http://www.ncl.org/anr/.

First Night® Turns New Year's Eve Into a Community Celebration Of The Arts

Nix the noisemakers ...
Put down that gun at midnight and ...
Can the Korbel ...
But do call First Night International in Boston and turn a tarnished tradition on its head by starting a First Night celebration on New Year's Eve — an alcohol-free, low-cost, culturally diverse celebration — and, in the process, building a new local legacy that will help reinvigorate a sense of community through a shared cultural experience.

FIRST NIGHT®
International

Initiated in 1976 "to recapture the symbolic significance of the passage from the old year to the new ... and to deepen and broaden the public's appreciation of the visual and performing arts," First Night New Year's Eve celebrations were held in 190 U.S. and 19 Canadian communities on December 31, 1997.

First Night is a registered trademark; communities must comply with their standards; there's an annual conference and there are fees and dues for a community to get involved. But the sheer number of participating communities reflects how it has been embraced as a most sensible and sane event to help keep communities pulling together rather than apart.

For information on how to start this New Year's Eve tradition in your community, contact First Night International, 200 Lincoln St., Ste. 301, Boston, MA 02111; call 617-357-0065 or visit their website at http://www.firstnightintl.org.

COMMUNITY #48

Build a Lifelong Line Of Defense Against Economic Jolts By "Building Learning Communities"

Every community, at one time or another, has been jolted by an unexpected plant shutdown, military base closing or some other blindsided business or government decision.

While companies come and go, community workers remain behind with mortgages, rents and car payments that keep coming.

NATIONAL LEAGUE OF CITIES

Aimed at buffering the disconnect period and keeping communities economically competitive in an increasingly volatile job market is a visionary guide from the National League of Cities (NLC) called *Building Learning Communities* ($5.00).

Pulling no punches, this one in a series of NLC Futures Reports rests the responsibility on communities to get ahead of the curve. "The stakes are enormous," it warned. "A community's capacity to provide a continuum of learning opportunities — from pre-school through retirement — may well be the critical determining factor in local economic growth in the years ahead."

The guide identifies 26 successful city or city-county collaborations with contact numbers for replication. Sample communities that developed the "human capacity" of public and private sector employees include:

- Building 21st Century Communities in Elkhart, IN and Genesee County, MI
- Intergenerational Learning Centers in Commerce City, CO
- Lifelong Learning Committee in Dearborn Heights, MI
- Skills Enhancement Program in Savannah, GA
- Transportation Careers Academy in Los Angeles, CA

For almost 75 years, the NLC has been encouraging full participation and continuous improvement for all city employees, not just at the top tier.

For a catalog of all of its practical publications and services, contact Public Affairs Dept., National League of Cities, 1301 Pennsylvania Ave., NW, Washington, DC 20004; call 202-626-3000 or visit their website at http://www.nlc.org.

Put "National Volunteer Events" On Your Community Calendar

To create a new tradition of "conspicuous caring," insist that National Volunteer Days, Weeks and Events are promoted *just like* Memorial Day or the Fourth of July.

If volunteer events are on community calendars in daily and weekly newspapers, flyers in libraries, your city's annual calendar and on city websites, people will get the message. Blending these events into local media will begin to build the layers of annual participation that will make them traditions.

Among many good ones, here are 8 volunteer-related events or holidays to weave into your community's consciousness:

- **Martin Luther King, Jr. Community Service Day**   Loretta King emphasizes that Americans should observe her husband's holiday by following Dr. King's philosophy that "everyone can be great because everyone can serve." In 1994, the King Holiday and Service Act designated the King Holiday as a national day of community service. Call 202-606-5000 or visit their website at http://www.nationalservice.org. *3rd Monday in January*

- **National Volunteer Week**   Established in 1974, this week is coordinated by the Points of Light Foundation to pay tribute to the backbone of our society: the selfless volunteer. Call 202-223-9186 for the focus on specific annual initiatives. *Usually 3rd Week in April*

- **Earth Day**   Now more than ever, this one day is needed to reinforce the absolute necessity of everyone taking action to create a healthy and clean environment for the survival of humans, plants and wildlife. Visit their website at http://www.sdearthtimes.com/edn/ for a state-by-state list of activities or call 212-922-0048. *April 22*

- **National Rebuilding Day**   Christmas In April is the leading volunteer organization that rehabilitates the homes of low-income elderly and disabled. Call 202-483-9083 to learn how to start a program in your hometown. *Usually last Saturday in April*

- **Stand for Children Day**   Originated in 1995, this new day encourages communities to focus on activities to ensure every child a healthy start, healthy development and healthy passage into adulthood. To receive a free organizer's kit, call 800-663-4032 or visit their website at http://www.stand.org. *June 1*

- **Red Ribbon Week**   As a symbolic tribute to a drug enforcement agent who was killed in Mexico, red ribbons were first worn in 1985 by angry parents and youth to draw awareness to the destruction of drugs and as a lasting commitment to keep kids drug-free. In 1988, the National Family Partnership sponsored the first National Red Ribbon Celebration. Call the Partnership for red ribbons, decals, stickers and other promotional materials at 314-845-1933. *Last week in October*

- **Make A Difference Day**   In 1992, USA WEEKEND in partnership with the Points of Light Foundation began promoting a national day of doing good deeds. It's gained momentum each year and now has over 1 million people contributing in their communities. Call 800-416-3824 for an information packet or visit their website at http://www.usaweekend.com. *4th Saturday in October*

- **National Philanthropy Day**   Founded by the National Society of Fund-Raising Executives, this event is a great way to salute local philanthropists. Call 800-666-FUND, ext. 452 for more information. *3rd Tuesday in November*

"KaBOOM!"
Works The Room
To Re-energize Community Playgrounds

A community catalyst dedicated solely to having safe and modern playgrounds with kids romping freely is a national nonprofit called KaBOOM!

Incorporated in 1995, KaBOOM! really knows how to help individuals and organizations work the "room" of community contacts for building playgrounds.

From a simple, 1-page application, KaBOOM! puts you into its Playground Pool — a database that links corporate and foundation funding to grassroots initiatives.

It then supports communities to gather all the key ingredients for a local success — playground architects, financial contributors, equipment manufacturers, project planning manuals, parks and recreation departments, neighborhood associations and "hands-on" technical glue — to mold your vision into action.

A project in Harlem was an extraordinary example of how community-built playgrounds can make a difference throughout a neighborhood. After a new playground and nearby parks were renovated, there was a 32% reduction in child admissions for major injuries to the Harlem Hospital.

Projects typically cost $40,000 to $50,000; take 5-12 months to plan and 1-4 days to build during the final "Playground Raising" stage.

To receive its Getting Started Kit, contact KaBOOM!, 2213 M St., NW, Ste. 200, Washington, DC 20037; call 888-789-PLAY or visit their website at http://www.kaboom.org.

"Store to Door"
Reduces One Big Chore

While most communities have a Meals On Wheels program, one community has creatively connected the dot on deliveries to older adults who still live and cook independently, but need a helping hand to bring home the bacon.

Called "Store to Door," this shopping and delivery service has been operating in Portland, OR since 1990.

Very simply, volunteers take shopping orders on Tuesdays; fill orders  at a Fred Meyer store and then deliver them to their 260 clients throughout the Portland metropolitan area. They also handle the paperwork; honor coupons; take back recyclables and put the food on the shelves.

While groceries are the primary request, other items such as prescriptions, household goods and an ongoing, caring connection are also delivered by the 100 volunteers in the program.

Volunteers range in age from 10-85 with all receiving priceless satisfaction in return for this much-needed service for fiercely-independent older adults.

For more information on how to adapt this multidimensional program to your hometown, contact Store to Door of Oregon, 2145 NW Overton St., Portland, OR 97210 or call 503-413-8223.

Afterschool Gardens Bleach Blight In Detroit & South Bronx

Turn off the afternoon talk shows and tune in to gardening a vacant lot with children if you want to plant the seeds of good citizenship and beautify your community at the same time.

"After we cleaned up a vacant lot and planted a garden, the litter really stopped," recalled Maureen Harrison, co-director of REACH (Revitalizing Education to Achieve a Climate of Hope), an afterschool program for homeless children and their families, in *Creative Living*.

"People who used to sit on benches and toss their bottles over the fence don't do that anymore, because they know the kids will be the ones to pick it up."

Harrison is convinced the garden has given the children a sense of control they wouldn't otherwise have in their lives. "Many of these kids have grown up powerless about where they live or where they eat," she added. "But the garden is *theirs*. They decide what to plant and where to plant it. And once we got out there, we were amazed by how the kids got involved, how they asked questions about insects and how things grow."

Harrison and her co-director, Natalie Cuchel, parlayed that interest into teaching other things like solving math problems to the basics of good nutrition.

For information on how to start a similar program in your community, contact REACH, 303 Greenwich St., New York, NY 10013 or call 212-349-8073.

========

Another similar program, known as **"The Gardening Angels,"** involves 600 older adults, young volunteers and school children. Instead of the proverbial lemonade stand, "The Cucumber Kids" sell their harvest on the streets. **For more information, contact The Gardening Angels, 4227 Mt. Elliott, Detroit, MI 48201.**

Petition, Lobby, Stomp-Your-Feet And Demand a "Graffiti Hotline" In Your Community!

Two of the most popular attractions in Southern California are Disneyland and Dodger Stadium.

Why? These places are clean-gene magnets. By keeping their attractions nearly spotless, they continually draw a steady stream of tourists as well as local residents.

Cleanliness is a very powerful, subconscious marketing motivator as to why people conduct repeat business at certain establishments.

In the last 20 years, however, the phenomenon of graffiti has reared its ugly aerosol head in one community after another. Graffiti carries a psychological blight as well as a visual one. Entire communities can disintegrate rapidly if graffiti creeps into a few neighborhoods. Surprisingly, many community leaders have neglected this very basic root problem and can't figure out why their towns are losing businesses.

Although surrounded by graffiti in nearby communities, my hometown of Burbank, CA has a "Graffiti Hotline" answering machine that records a resident's sighting of a recent outbreak. Within 7 days (often sooner), the offensive scribbling is removed by a crew which uses the appropriate paint to cover up the former eyesore.

Naturally, the graffiti taggers are never empowered by their juvenile markings as the exposure is an ephemeral one. By creating a graffiti-free atmosphere and combining it with other community attributes, Burbank continues to be a desirable place to live and work.

Don't let the cancer of graffiti spread through your community. Make it a part of the city charter for there will be no community redevelopment projects if graffiti has a grip. For lasting economic survival, get a "Graffiti Hotline" up and running tomorrow!

Hometown Murals
Raise Morale & Money

In 1983, the logging community of Chemainus, British Columbia was lagging badly.

It just lost its sawmill, the town's primary source of employment.

But rejuvenation came via Romania.

On a trip to that Eastern bloc country, Karl Schutz saw how large, outdoor murals had dramatically changed local communities. He brought the mural movement back to Chemainus and re-wrote the town's history.

From roughly 40 businesses and 5 empty stores, Chemainus recovered nicely with over 300 new businesses and 400,000 tourists a year after painting the town with 32 murals.

Other communities such as Eureka, Lompoc and Twentynine Palms, CA; Vale, OR and Enumclaw, WA have all grasped the mural baton and picked up their collective spirits by allowing local artists to express themselves on huge local canvases.

Hometown Murals — a morale-booster that pays dividends!

Photo courtesy of Eureka/Humboldt County Convention & Visitors Bureau

Hold a Community "Open House For The Arts"

Something dramatic must be done in communities to drive culture into the forefront of the public's awareness and, ideally, into greater public participation.

That something could be an all out, all day, community-wide "Open House For The Arts" that's well publicized and offers free access to the public.

On October 4, 1997, Southern California held its "3rd Annual Los Angeles County-Wide Arts Open House" with more than 100 arts organizations from low brow to high brow including opera, theatre, museums, libraries, the Philharmonic, the Master Chorale and the Thelonius Monk Jazz Ensemble among dozens of others. In all, there were 7 centers of activity inviting the public to come, browse and sample the wide variety of cultural fare.

Some groups had as much as 100% increases in attendance over a normal Saturday.

What would it take to pull this together in your community to get people motivated to make the arts a habit rather than an occasional outing?

Establish a
"Disaster-Recovery Sister City"

The Oklahoma City bombing left 168 people dead.

The Red River flooding left 50,000 people homeless.

The Jarrell tornado flattened that Texas community into a tortilla.

In all these tragedies, *Disaster* meant desolation and despair to entire communities.

Also, in these cases, *Recovery* was often slow, staggered and inadequate. (Although 20,000 volunteers did come from all across the country to help the people who lived along the Red River in Grand Forks, ND, we can't assume that every disaster will receive that kind of support.)

Whether it's the hand of man or the quirks of Mother Nature, every community (including yours) is vulnerable to a disaster.

While the American Red Cross rushes in and provides much needed band-aid relief for a few weeks to assist the exhausted local public agencies, a month later there is the physical and mental recovery that needs to be coordinated by people who are still not in a coping mode.

Why not establish a *"Disaster-Recovery Sister City"* exchange plan where communities of similar size e.g. Stockton, CA with a population of 233,000 is linked with Akron, OH which has the same approximate population?

Disaster-Recovery teams from each city would be ready to leap into action with immediate back-up support personnel and recovery plans to restore the economic and psychological health of the community much more quickly than by relying on traditional resources.

Take Cab Drivers To Your Chamber Of Commerce Luncheons

A single experience will dictate a lifetime opinion.

Ask a person about their trip to Anywhere, USA and usually one moment will stick out, sometimes an unpleasant encounter.

In every community, cab drivers are the unofficial PR Hosts for the town. What they say and how they treat a visitor can have a direct impact on that person spreading good will or ill will about a community.

A creative cabbie communications program in Erie, PA could easily be adapted to any community.

Their program coordinates the arrival of out of town visitors to their respective hotels. When a cab driver picks up the arriving guests at the airport, he asks his customers where they're staying.

The driver then calls the dispatcher who in turn calls the hotel to verify the reservation and to make sure everything is in order. This creates a very pleasant chain of courteous concern that later becomes a treasured souvenir visitors take back to their hometowns.

Why not take it one step further?

At Chamber of Commerce luncheons and mixers, invite cab drivers as regular guests. Tell them they are the "official" front-line everyday ambassadors for the community. Make them feel completely appreciated as their contacts with visitors are very crucial to the quality of life in your community.

PART II

Business

Every business in every industry has an obligation to give back to the communities from where it earns its profits. It's one of the oldest laws of common decency: When you take, you reciprocate.

In Chapter 6 titled "Do What You Do Best For The Communities You Serve ... " there are 29 innovative programs from large corporations to consultants to Main Street retail enterprises in a variety of industries. They all give textbook examples of how business people are giving back what comes naturally to them — their skills, services or products.

These 29 are presented to challenge competitors in the respective industries to create their own projects or to inspire like-minded individuals in other industries to get involved by starting meaningful programs for their local schools and communities.

In Chapter 7 titled "Portable Ideas For Small to Large Businesses," there are 18 creative and adaptable ideas or established nonprofit business alliances that any size business can initiate or contact to begin a commitment to a specific mission.

========

These combined 47 ideas, programs and partnerships are designed to stimulate all levels of business to make innovative community and public school contributions so not only can more citizens have an equal footing as we enter the 21st Century but also business can make a long-term investment in its future by being a more balanced corporate citizen.

CHAPTER 6

Do What You Do Best For The Communities You Serve ...

Business

BUSINESS #1

If You're In Transportation, Give It Up For Some Free Rides!

Reach out and transport someone ...

If you work in the transportation industry — airline, auto, bus, rail, taxi, moving van, ferry, cruise or horse-drawn carriage — you can help make it a small world after all by giving a lift to those in need.

One such worthwhile organization is AirLifeLine, a group of volunteer pilots, which takes seriously ill people to places where they can receive special medical attention.

Or offer a program similar to Southwest Airlines' annual "Home For the Holidays" promotion. Since 1979, Southwest has given over 10,000 older adults the chance to share the holidays in destinations that normally would have been financially unreachable. Its program provides each recipient with a complimentary round-trip ticket to any Southwest Airlines destination. All recipients are at least 65 years of age and live on a fixed income. For the 1996 holiday season, the airline flew over 850 older adults to visit friends or loved ones. Other exemplary programs include American Airlines' "Miles For Kids In Need" which matches donated

frequent flyer miles from passengers so needy kids can fly free for medical treatment; Federal Express which transports American Red Cross emergency equipment to national disaster sites; Greyhound's "Operation: Home Free" which gives free rides home to runaway teenagers and Apartment Movers of Lincoln, NE which offers free moving services to women trying to break free of abusive relationships.

But every transportation company should implement some form of this compassionate concept as a natural outreach to help people reconnect or re-establish their lives. The good will of transporting people, equipment, services or furniture can be immeasurable.

For more information about AirLifeLine and how their program operates, contact AirLifeLine, 6133 Freeport Blvd., Sacramento, CA 95822 or call 800-446-1231.

========

A related community nonprofit program is the Women's Transit Authority in Madison, WI that provides rape-prevention rides at night and trips to medical appointments during the day for women and their children who live within a 4-mile radius of downtown Madison.

For more information, contact the Women's Transit Authority, 333 W. Mifflin St., Madison, WI 53703 or call 608-256-3710.

Home Depot Hammers Away At Rebuilding Communities With $38+ Million In Community Grants & Projects

A nuts-and-bolts example of doing what's best for the communities it serves, Home Depot is a natural born leader in the home improvement field. Hands down.

Since 1989, this Atlanta-based company has distributed $38+ million in community grants and projects in 3 areas:

- Affordable Housing
- Environment
- Youth At-Risk

Perhaps even more remarkable is not just the money but the countless months and years of volunteer sweat equity that its employees — known as Team Depot — donate to build these projects and raise the spirits of the less fortunate in their communities. Also, if employees want to make financial contributions to nonprofits they can receive matching gifts up to $500.

Here is a potpourri of Home Depot projects:

- Funding over 100 Housing organizations
- Funding over 100 Youth organizations
- Funding over 100 Environmental organizations
- Partnerships with 147 Habitat For Humanity affiliates
- Partnerships with 58 Christmas In April affiliates
- 400+ associates volunteering to build HomeSafe in South Florida with many vendors donating supplies

Unlike many companies, Home Depot is not bashful about being an up front socially responsible company. Its mission: "To become a better corporate citizen redefines itself every day as we constantly look for new and creative ways to enhance the quality of life in all of our cities and towns, and in fact, the world."

For more information on its "Community Investment Guidelines," contact Community Affairs, Home Depot, 2455 Paces Ferry Rd., Atlanta, GA 30339 or call 770-433-8211.

International Paper Restores Faith & Rebuilds Churches By Donating $2+ Million In Lumber & Building Materials

One of the most wretched and smoldering remnants of our past is the lingering racism that continually flares up as we approach the 21st Century.

Nowhere was this more apparent than in the rural South from 1994-1996 when 124 churches were totaled or damaged by arsonists.

These heinous acts lit a counterfire under International Paper's Chairman John T. Dillon. In an employee memo, he declared that these "small towns and small-town values have long been part of our history …" and "This link, together with the premium we place on corporate citizenship, requires that International Paper respond in this time of need." And respond they did.

International Paper gave the National Council of Churches a blank check for building materials — beams, flooring, walls, sheeting, siding, shingles, doors and countertops — so that every church that had not been rebuilt not only got what they needed but they also got the materials delivered within a week.

Through 1997, International Paper has provided the materials to rebuild *28 churches*. Over $2 million in lumber and building materials (at wholesale prices) have been donated to the massive effort. In addition, International Paper matched $37,787 in employee contributions for a cash donation of $75,574 directly to the National Council of Churches.

Why can't more global companies like International Paper put "a premium on corporate citizenship" by creatively stepping up to the plate and providing core products and services to those in immediate need from acts of natural or man-made destruction?

Do what you do best for the communities that make you profitable. It's that simple.

MONEY Magazine Provides 10 Months Of Free Financial Advice To Entire Community

Instead of a lavish 25th Anniversary party, *MONEY* Magazine threw an adoption party for a typical U.S. city — Elgin, IL, a self-sufficient community of 85,000.

From January to October, 1997, the magazine's best minds conducted free-of-charge monthly seminars on retirement, investment and tax-planning and held career and basic financial guidance classes for students in the Elgin schools. Also, 10,000 free subscriptions were distributed and a personal Elgin website — **www.pathfinder.com/money/elgin** — was available if anyone wanted to e-mail a question into the project.

With financial support from Fidelity Investments, *MONEY*, in all, spent $2 million on the most ambitious magazine project of its kind.

What if other publications such as *Prevention, PC World, National Geographic* or any number of other worthy magazines did similar community adoptions? Literally 100s of hometowns could be uplifted with these hands-on, "living magazine" education programs.

MONEY has also offered to work with any organization that wants to adapt what they learned from this project.

For more information, contact "Elgin Project," *MONEY* Magazine, Time & Life Building, Rockefeller Center, New York, NY 10020 or call 212-522-1212.

Westin Hotels Adopts a Homeless Shelter Turn This Light On!

In nearly every community, there are many hotels and motels such as Best Western, Days Inn, Holiday Inn, Radisson and Westin among others. Also, in nearly every community, there are homeless shelters.

What if the "for profit" innkeepers started assisting the "nonprofit" innkeepers?

Since hotels and motels specialize in giving travelers a refreshing respite and sending them on their way, they are natural candidates to adopt and freshen up homeless shelters with their expertise.

Associates of the Westin Hotel in Cincinnati, OH did just that by adopting the City Gospel Mission and cooking hot meals for 130 homeless people; refurbishing the pantry; donating clothes and *hiring* a homeless man as a cook.

If this kind of hotel/motel adoption were applied in every hometown, it would not only raise the spirits of the volunteers running the shelters but it would also give some of the homeless people a way out of their plight. Or the hotels and motels in a community could share the responsibility on a rotating basis, say every 6 months.

So if you're in the hospitality industry, or if you know someone who is, present them with this heads up idea of hotel/motel adoptions of homeless shelters and turn this light on, far and wide!

========

In a somewhat similar vein, Marriott introduced its "Pathways to Independence" program in 1991. It enlists welfare recipients through a rigorous job training program. Approximately 300 out of 750 "graduates" are still working for Marriott.

3 Newspapers Share $25,000 Pew Award By Shifting From "Detachment To Community Re-engagement"

Recognizing that daily newspapers can no longer be mere scorekeepers of crime, sports and stocks, the Pew Center For Civic Journalism has raised its industry's consciousness by honoring newspapers that are redefining journalism "from the citizens up."

In 1996, the first 3 winners of the James K. Batten Awards for Excellence in Civic Journalism included:

- *Argus Leader*, Sioux Falls, SD, for "A Community on the Rise"
- *The Charlotte Observer* for "Taking Back Our Neighborhoods"
- *The Kansas City Star* for "Raising Kansas City"

While most newspapers typically run either a 3 or 5-part series on a specific topic, *The Kansas City Star*, for example, devoted a year and more than 50 reporters and editors who wrote and thoroughly **Pew Center for Civic Journalism** examined a value a month that was most important to instill in children. With over 200 stories filed, 1000s of citizens participated in workshops on children's literature, discipline and self-esteem.

"The winning entries all illuminate the basic attribute of civic journalism: Doing journalism in a manner calculated to re-engage people in the process of public life," defined the Batten Advisory Board.

"The common thread is that each of these entries demonstrated the impact journalism can have when it moves beyond detachment and the mere chronicling of problems. They gave citizens a way to have a different kind of conversation with each other and to connect with each other in new, more deliberative and useful ways."

For more information on how these papers creatively redefined their reportorial coverage, contact the Pew Center for Civic Journalism, 1101 Connecticut Ave., NW, Ste. 420, Washington, DC 20036 or call 202-331-3200.

========

Local papers which simply want to re-connect by holding a community event might want to consider tapping into the success of a small Wisconsin newspaper.

After a negative segment on Wausau, WI appeared on "60 Minutes," the *Wausau Daily Herald* convinced 200 businesses and organizations to sponsor a "Random Acts of Kindness" Week from March 13-18, 1995.

While newspaper employees went out in "Kindness Squads" performing spontaneous deeds, bank employees washed car windows in drive-up lanes; church groups mowed lawns; movie theatres gave out free passes to people waiting in line and an individual walked into a restaurant and said, "Coffee on the house for everyone!"

On the newspaper hot line, more than 500 calls were received from people who had witnessed acts of kindness. Banners, balloons, bookmarks and buttons were all distributed throughout the community creating a truly kind atmosphere.

What simple act would it take to get your hometown newspaper to run a similar campaign to re-energize your community?

For more information, contact *Wausau Daily Herald,* 800 Scott St., Wausau, WI 54402 or call 715-842-2101.

"ChildSpree"
Mervyn's Rings In School Year By Helping Children Dress For Success

What's a new school year without new clothes?

Although middle-class parents do their annual grousing — knowing the hit on their credit card statements in September will be jarring — what about parents who can't afford much more than a new knapsack?

To defray their costs and to impart self-esteem in the hearts and minds of needy children, Mervyn's California and its 275  nationwide stores implemented a novel "ChildSpree" program that enables kids 6-18 to go on shopping sprees worth $50 to $100 of school clothes.

Since 1993, nearly 50,000 kids across the country have obtained new duds. The children are selected by organizations such as the Boys and Girls Club, Kiwanis and The Salvation Army. Each group contributes up to $2000 which is matched by $2000 from the local Mervyn's California store for a total of $4000 in fashion funds. The chosen children are then guided by an adult chaperon when they go on their shopping spree.

"When kids go back to school without new clothes, it can lead to self-esteem problems that prevent them from learning to their full potential," explained Mervyn's spokesperson Carol Johnson. "We're in the apparel business and we thought this would be a good way to contribute to children's education."

Since 1993, Foot Locker has also offered free "Back to School" packages with new shoes, clothes and supplies for inner-city youth. If you retail clothes for children or you know a retailer in your hometown who does, why not start a similar program?

What a difference it could make if every community had retailers and nonprofit organizations working together to help students with a snazzier outlook for the school year.

"HAIR CLUB For Kids"
Gives Children With Cancer a New Head Of Self-Esteem

"In some cases of children with cancer, I have seen kids appear to be more devastated over their hair loss than from having cancer," explained Lisa Tavitian, director of HAIR CLUB For Kids.

"I believe this is because hair loss is a constant reminder that they are sick. Hair loss also contributes to children developing a low self-esteem as their peers don't understand the effects of cancer. Friends then begin to make fun of those changes in appearance."

Helping kids with cancer cope with unwanted ridicule and give back a sense of their self-worth is HAIR CLUB For Kids, a benevolent outgrowth of HAIR CLUB For Men. It will design and fit a natural-looking system that matches the color, curl, density and size of the child's head — at no charge — for any child ages 6-18 who has lost 50% of his or her hair from any form of cancer.

Ideally parents should submit locks of their child's hair to make the system. But even if a child has lost all of his or her hair, every kid can still receive a custom-fitted hair piece.

Besides saving the family $2000-$3000 for the cost of the restoration, more importantly it helps eliminate the downtime of depression kids endure and restores their self-esteem as they struggle through the physical side of recovery.

Parents of kids with cancer can call 800-HAIR-CLUB for the location nearest their home. For written inquiries, contact HAIR CLUB For Kids, 441 Lexington Ave., Ste. 1211, New York, NY 10017.

Weight Watchers' Members Shed Pounds; Give Business Suits To Women Entering Job Market

Lose those pounds ... and shed those clothes!

That's the meeting mantra that took place at Weight Watchers across Washington, DC, Maryland and Virginia in the fall of 1995.

Over 4000 pieces of professional attire were collected in 90 days and donated to a local nonprofit agency called "Suited for Change." It in turn outfitted women who completed job training programs and were seeking full-time employment.

The clothes campaign was so successful Suited for Change even received a box of winter clothing from a woman in California.

This perfect ensemble — women who are feeling good about themselves as they lower their clothes size and women who are raising their standards with their "new" suits — is a most sensible community program that could easily be adopted by other weight reduction clinics and companies selling weight-loss products and services across the U.S.

For more information, contact Weight Watchers, 11119 Rockville Pike, Ste. 209, Rockville, MD 20852 or call 301-770-4115.

Hospitals Can Become "Homework Helpers" For Kids After School

Outside of genetics, 3 to 6 p.m. is probably the most critical time in shaping the character of our youth.

They either fall under the influence of wayward peers; stay involved with afterschool activities or meander to home alone. According to a survey by the Child Welfare League of America, as many as 77% of U.S. 3rd graders are spending time by themselves at home.

To help keep kids connected after the school day ends, 2 hospitals have set up similar Afterschool Phone Lines.

- In Glendale, CA, "PhoneFriend" was arranged by the Glendale Adventist Medical Center. In 1995, 8 adult volunteers and 7 high school students answered over 15,000 calls from frightened or bored kids needing a friend to talk to.

- In San Diego, CA, "Children's Line 10" is a hot-line for elementary school latchkey kids. It's operated by the San Diego Children's Hospital.

What if every community had a conscientious hospital or business taking the initiative to coordinate this afterschool telementoring of help, hope and trust?

ADT Distributes Electronic Safety Accessory For Abused Women In 124+ Communities

Almost 4 million women are battered by almost 4 million men in the U.S. every year.

Now finally devoid of the euphemism "family dispute," spousal abuse has at long last moved up in the priority chain at local Police Departments. It's also become more of a focused issue in the court system, District Attorney's office and community shelters as many progressive changes have been implemented.

Yet the problem will continue into the 21st Century.

"Try reaching the phone when you have an animal coming at you," vividly described one woman in *The New York Times*.

Giving a more immediate link of protection when a woman sees such imminent danger is ADT Security Services, Inc. It offers complimentary electronic security pendants for approximately 15 women at high risk in each of more than 124 communities across the U.S. Normally, ADT commits $50,000 per community over a 5-year period.

When activated by a button on either side of the device, the pendant zaps an electronic signal to an ADT monitoring center which in turn relays it to the local Police Department where dispatchers are sensitized to its high priority status.

ADT's AWARE program (Abused Women's Active Response Emergency) has been credited with helping to save the lives of 25 women since its inception in 1992.

For more information on this natural electronic extension into the communities it serves, contact AWARE, ADT Security Services, Inc., 14200 E. Exposition Ave., Aurora, CO 80012.

BUSINESS #12

"Sharing the Care"
Pfizer Fills a Need For Working Poor By Filling Free Prescriptions At 340+ Community Health Centers

With 41 million people lacking health insurance in the U.S., the working poor often suffer in silence from an inability to pay for basic medications.

That's why Pfizer's award-winning "Sharing the Care" program is such a standout in this era of tight-fisted managed care.

Very simply, the program helps the working poor who fall below the federal poverty level and have no private insurance or public assistance covering pharmaceuticals.

Since November, 1993, Pfizer has filled over 2.1 million prescriptions — at no charge — valued at $102 million for its top-of-the-line medications for everything from hypertension to depression to diabetes and everything

in between. They're dispensed through a network of more than 340 federally qualified community, migrant and homeless health centers.

Developed in partnership with the National Governors' Association and the National Association of Community Health Centers, Sharing the Care is the only drug access program of its kind.

While Pfizer has taken the lead, Sharing the Care should be a trip wire to others in the vast health care industry to do just that, i.e. share the *cost* of care for those less fortunate.

For more information on how this program works, contact "Sharing the Care," Pfizer Inc, 235 East 42nd St., New York, NY 10017 or call 800-984-1500.

=======

A related but smaller program is SmithKline Beecham's $10,000 Healthy Start/Healthy Future Community Organizing grants designed to help individual communities help children (who are medically underserved and at-risk) eliminate barriers preventing them from seeking adequate care.

For more information, contact Community Partnership, SmithKline Beecham, One Franklin Plaza, P.O. Box 7929, Philadelphia, PA 19101 or call 215-751-7024.

"Volunteers In Medicine Clinic"
Doctor Instills Outbreak Of Caring

As many of the 170,000 retired doctors in the U.S. are discovering, golf has its limits. But taking another course, a few are also discovering that volunteering does not.

At the same time, they're also part of a growing chorus chafing at how managed care has turned their compassionate profession into such a vicious vortex where patients have to go before HMO appeal boards to seek treatments that they or their employers are already paying for! Let alone the 41 million uninsured people in the U.S. who have little recourse for their basic health care needs.

But along came Dr. Jack B. McConnell of Hilton Head Island, SC who is not only putting sanity and soul back into his profession but he's also creating a nationwide model that could put holistic humanity back into this gyrating juggernaut that is sorely lacking in morals and ethics.

Very simply, in June, 1994, Dr. McConnell opened a debt-free, 7000 sq.ft. health care center with no fees for service. The Volunteers in Medicine Clinic is now staffed by 44 volunteer retired doctors (many of whom are specialists in their field), 51 volunteer retired nurses and community volunteers who are all free of streaming paper trails.

Run by a few paid employees who dispense not only free medical care — covering the full range of health problems found in a typical primary care clinic as well as dental services, social and psychological counseling — the clinic also delivers respect for the individual as the staff refers to each and every person who walks in the door as a "friend" or "neighbor."

What a powerful prescription for raising the standards of health care for the local working poor. For treating an average of 87 neighbors a day, it only costs $1800 a day for overhead or about $21 each.

In addition, the center has created savings of $350,000 to $500,000 per year for the local 68-bed hospital as the uninsured go straight to the clinic instead of the nearby ER.

Since its inception, similar clinics have opened in Erie, PA; Wooster, OH; Newark and Dover, NJ; Mound, MO; Portland, ME; Columbus, IN and Stuart, FL with others planned for New Orleans, LA and Brownsville, TX. Dr. McConnell is also creating a "Start-Up Manual" to assist several hundred towns which have requested information on how to replicate clinics in their communities.

If there were a strong nationwide chain of such volunteer clinics employing a good percentage of the 170,000 retired doctors as well as offering internships for new doctors, it could perhaps put pressure on the prevailing tactics of managed care to relinquish their hypocritical ways and return to the Hippocratic oath.

For more information, contact Volunteers In Medicine Clinic, 15 Northridge Dr., Hilton Head Island, SC 29925 or call 803-681-6612.

Health Care Professionals Donate Services To Help People Look Better, Eat, Walk & See

Sometimes, it's just a simple gesture of providing basic health care that can help propel people in need with the desire to succeed.

For example:

- Fresh Start Surgical Gifts in Encinitas, CA offered free cosmetic surgery — caused by birth defects, abuse or accidents — to children whose parents couldn't afford the treatment.

- Dentist Duane Schmidt of Cedar Rapids, IA started the "Doctors With a Heart" program whereby one day a year he treats over 170 people who can't afford dental care.

- Podiatrist Pamela Leavitt of Northridge, CA held a drive for Imelda Marcos types to donate shoes to help people get back on their feet.

- Opticians and staff from LensCrafters have given free eye care or lenses to over 50,000 people worldwide. "Our goal," stated CEO David Browne, "is to hand deliver the gift of sight to one million needy people by the year 2003."

If you are a health care professional — such as a dermatologist; chiropractor; ear, nose and throat doctor; plastic surgeon or from any other health care specialty — consider offering a free day or co-sponsoring an event in your hometown to give the less fortunate a needed lift in life.

"Pet Placement Program"
Pet Shop Owners Can Help Older Adults Reduce Doctor Visits

You may not think owning a Sheltie or a Cocker Spaniel is a way to reduce the cost of health care. But think again.

A UCLA study of 938 people over 65 (who were covered by Medicare and enrolled in an HMO) found that *37% of the pet people* made fewer visits to their doctor.

An even more startling confirmation comes from the health records of 169 individuals following a heart attack. Although 20 out of the 169 died within a year, *only one* of the fatalities occurred among 87 individuals who owned a dog.

Other possible wellness benefits include a reduction in blood pressure, anxiety and a general boosting of spirits.

So if you're a pet shop or pet supply owner, consider implementing a pet placement program for older adults in your hometown.

========

Since 1984, Ralston Purina Company has conducted a cat/canine campaign called "The Purina Pets For People Program." It partners with participating humane organizations to offer, free of charge, companion pets to qualified adults 60 years of age and older. The unique program covers the cost of adoption fees, pet supplies, nutritional information, product coupons and a starter supply of dog or cat food.

Since its inception, the program has helped more than 80,000 pets find caring companions and donated more than $9.2 million to participating animal shelters.

For more information on Pets For People, contact Ralston Purina Company, Checkerboard Square, St. Louis, MO 63164 or call 314-982-1348.

========

Or contact The Delta Society — a nonprofit organization that promotes animals as a way of helping people improve their health, independence and quality of life — by calling for their free brochure listing services and publications at 800-869-6898.

"Communities On Phone Patrol — COPP"
Cellular Telecommunications Program Arms Community Watch Groups With 50,000 Cellular Phones

High technology is touching down at the grass roots level, thanks to the Cellular Telecommunications Industry Association.

Neighborhood Watch and community patrol groups can receive a free cellular phone (and free air time) that's pre-programmed to a specific emergency response number chosen by the local volunteer group and local law enforcement agency.

Called "Communities on Phone Patrol" or COPP, the program fuses volunteerism with wireless technology. In some neighborhoods, the use of cellular phones by community watch groups has decreased crime by as much as 70%.

The Community Policing Consortium — a partnership of 5 of the leading police organizations — is screening and coordinating the COPP program. They have a 1-page application for police agencies to distribute to local Community Watch groups.

Could other communications industry associations donate technology products to social service organizations which desperately need to upgrade their technology? Or if you're a member of such an association, why not come up with a suggestion to your national headquarters?

For an application to receive a phone for your Community Watch program, first contact your local police agency or the Consortium at 800-833-3085 or contact the Cellular Telecommunications Industry, 1250 Connecticut Ave., NW, Ste. 200, Washington, DC 20036 or call 202-785-0081.

Radio Stations Plug Into Community Participation

Always a very personal medium, a radio station is usually selected for one or more of the following reasons:

- Music
- Sports
- News

- Traffic
- Weather
- Venting

Raising the ante, touching an untapped nerve and bringing more social responsibility to the digital turntable, Power KPWR in Los Angeles added a new bullet to the fiercely-competitive air waves:

- Community Participation

But it just wasn't a seasonal toy drive. This radio station earned its street credibility in meaningful and lasting ways.

Hispanic-oriented KPWR produced and sold CDs that, in turn, raised $300,000 and free air time for a local Learning Center in addition to raising $210,000 for on-the-job training programs for local disadvantaged youth.

========

- Another Southern California station, KLOS, has held its "You're So Vein" blood drive for 15 years which annually has contributed over 2500 pints of blood to the American Red Cross.

- And in Davenport, IA, entrepreneur Terry Lunardi linked forces with local radio station KLJG enabling a group of 5th graders to run their own "on-the-air" radio station at their elementary school. Just imagine a beaming parent listening to a son or daughter on the radio.

If you're employed in radio; if you know someone in radio or if you're a motivated fan of a station, why not initiate similar participation programs that can firmly entrench and expand listener loyalty within your community?

"H.U.G.S."
New Orleans-Based Law Firm
Files Barrage Of Good Will Briefs

At the legal firm of Adams and Reese, the defense for their communities never rests.

Since 1988, this atypical firm and 125 of its staff of 500 employees with offices in 6 cities have created a barrage of good will briefs "focused on the needy people of the community, not just institutions."

Called H.U.G.S. — **H**ope, **U**nderstanding, **G**iving, **S**upport — this community service program is a 1-to-1, small miracle project planned independently by each office.

A sample of H.U.G.S. events includes:

- Annual Halloween Carnival for Big Buddy kids
- Camp Challenge for kids with cancer
- Crawfish Boil & Talent Show for substance abuse house
- Easter Egg Hunt for abused children
- End of School Bowling party for abused children
- 5 Bingos a year for recovering stroke victims and Alzheimer's patients
- Kiss a Pig Fundraiser for diabetes
- Livestock Show & Rodeo for scholarships
- Pediatric AIDS events
- $75,000 playground refurbishing

Although Adams and Reese has attempted to enlist other law firms to start similar campaigns, the reaction has been lethargic at best. Which is interesting.

Since people in the legal field have to grasp difficult concepts, it's perplexing why such a simple, consistent community campaign is such a hurdle for other law firms to adopt and implement. While the hours spent in the community are not "billable," they will pay dividends far beyond the bottom line.

To file a discovery on this top-notch community program, contact H.U.G.S., c/o Adams and Reese, 4500 One Shell Square, New Orleans, LA 70139 or call 504-581-3234.

BUSINESS #19

Long-Haul Truckers Send Postcards; Students Learn Geography, History & Writing Skills

Long-distance truckers can deliver more than just America's cars, computers, food, gas, lumber and videos.

One innovative trucking company — Auto Transport Co. of Gardena, CA — figured since their drivers had windows to the outside world they could bring a realistic perspective into the classroom via their multiple destinations around the U.S.

A novel "Postcard Program" was coordinated with the Serrania Avenue School in Woodland Hills, CA. One 5th grade class received dozens of postcards from 3 of Auto Transport's coast-to-coast truckers. In return, the students sent bags of letters to the truckers at company headquarters.

"They learned so much," reported 5th grade teacher Meredith Smith in the *Daily News*. "They learned about geography, U.S. history, the capitols of states, communication — it's really hands-on learning. They were so excited about it. Everyday they would ask, 'Did we get a postcard?'"

Wal-Mart has a similar postcard program called "Trucker Buddy." But where are the 1000s of other independent and company truckers who could also easily send a steady stream of postcards back to their hometown schools to inspire and help educate local children with their "on the road" visual reports and experiences?

Photographer Hans Gutknecht/Los Angeles Daily News

Car Dealer Delivers
For Salvation Army

Think of the 1000s of car dealers and 1000s of idle service bays at those dealerships.

Now think of the 1000s of dilapidated vehicles owned by nonprofit organizations that need to be serviced.

Well the Dodge-Chrysler-Plymouth-Jeep-Eagle dealer of Vacaville, CA did just that and put them together.

When they heard that the local chapter of The Salvation Army had 2 out-of-service 1968 vans, it not only had its mechanics get the vans up and running but it also filled them with canned goods and winter clothes.

What a natural yet creative way for an auto dealership to literally service its community.

Now just imagine if car dealers in every community took it upon themselves to regularly maintain the vehicles of Meals On Wheels, American Red Cross and other mobile organizations that rely on day-to-day transportation.

It would be a tremendous lift for keeping these organizations and their drivers up and running safely and without costly mechanical delays.

"Volunteer Accountants" Get Those Calculators Clicking For Their Communities

Whether you're a member of a "Big Six" accounting firm or just a sole practitioner, you can punch in some big numbers as a volunteer in your community.

Designed for nonprofit organizations and individuals who need but can't afford professional accounting services, Accountants for the Public Interest (API) and its 22 nationwide affiliates annually donate more than 55,000 hours of service.

For example:

- Volunteer accountants with the Indiana affiliate helped 10,550 households receive more than $6 million in tax refunds and credits.

- Volunteer accountants with the Illinois affiliate provided 1-stop financial services for families and businesses impacted by the 1994 Mississippi River flood.

So if you're a company bookkeeper, sole practitioner or corporate accountant, here's a way you can balance the financial statements for nonprofits or others in need and make a conscientious statement for your community.

For more information on this most accountable organization, contact API, 1012 14th St., NW, Ste. 906, Washington, DC 20005 or call 202-347-1668.

"Kids Cafe"
Restaurants Can Become an Afternoon Delight For Hungry Children

It's 4 p.m. on any school day in the U.S.

There are 13 million hungry children out there who may also be part of the latchkey generation.

It's 4 p.m. in a restaurant, the slowest hour of the day, and the owner has an unfulfilled community spirit. Voila!

Many of these hungry children go to Boys & Girls Clubs, YMCAs and Community Service Centers which have programs with local food banks. Community-spirited restaurant owners and food service companies can augment these food programs by initiating a "Kids Cafe."

An extension of Second Harvest — the national network of nearly 200 food banks — Kids Cafe serves wholesome meals exclusively to needy children. While most of the items on the menu come from the local Second Harvest food banks, restaurants and food service companies can supplement the meals with their own culinary specialties. In addition, they can help in other areas of a child's development such as having guest chefs provide mentoring and tutoring.

If this sounds like a worthwhile recipe for your hometown, contact Second Harvest, 116 S. Michigan Ave., Ste. 4, Chicago, IL 60603; call 800-532-FOOD, 312-263-2303 or visit their website at http:// www.secondharvest.org.

========

Another way restaurants and catering companies can connect in their communities is by immediately donating their perishable leftovers to established soup kitchens, shelters, rehab centers and emergency feeding programs through one of the 190 programs of America Harvest.

For more information, contact America Harvest, Inc., 4 International Dr., Ste. 310, Rye Brook, NY 10573 or call 914-933-5741.

========

Representing 400,000 restaurants, the National Restaurant Association recently published a 60-page guide titled *A Restaurant Guide to Food Donation* to encourage its members "to be good community citizens" by distributing unused food.

For more information, call 202-331-5900.

Bloomington's Building Trades Council Nails Down Community Respect With Projects Built On The House

Eternally embroiled in adversarial relationships with architects, city building inspectors and property owners, organized labor typically has a feisty reputation.

But in Bloomington, IL, Local 99 has completely retrofitted that image.

By donating their construction skills; coaxing lumberyards and suppliers to provide building materials and attending city agency meetings, the Livingston and McLean Counties Building and Construction Trades Council (AFL-CIO) has won a Presidential Service Award, a Recognition Day from the Mayor and a leadership position in the construction industry for doing so many "on the house" community construction projects.

"It's taken our usual tough bricklayer or ironworker out of the doldrums," explained Rick Terven, Local 99's business manager. "Everyone has a more positive attitude. We're there because we care and you can see the changes you as an individual can make by having a positive attitude."

A few of their projects include: a new addition for the American Red Cross; a cancer laboratory used by 2 hospitals; small service repairs for older adults; remodeling homes for disabled and "Poetry Place," an outdoor stage for low-income families. The latter effort became one of their premiere projects employing the volunteer services of over 100 union craftsmen.

For more information on how this leading Local is rebuilding its community, contact Rick Terven, Livingston and McLean Counties Building and Construction Trades Council, 406 Eldorado Rd., Bloomington, IL 61704 or call 309-663-2337.

========

Another community-minded group active in rebuilding local communities is the National Association of Women in Construction. One particular chapter — which was recognized by the "Make a Difference Day" Campaign — rehabilitated a drug treatment center for female addicts in Honolulu, HI.

BUSINESS #24

"Penny Project"
Coast Federal Banks On The Future

How do you get children to understand the value of saving money in a participatory way?

How can cash-strapped schools find the funds to purchase modern computer equipment?

The answer to both: Get your school and community to collect 1,000,000 pennies.

When 4th grade teacher Kay Rich at the Leona Cox Elementary School in Canyon Country, CA was reading over her new math book to prepare for the 1995-96 school year, she landed on a year-long project of trying to collect a million of something.

"Who in the world came up with this hair-brained idea?" she asked. Rich then flipped to the last chapter and learned that the publisher of the math book really didn't expect anyone to do it. "That bothered me," Rich recalled. "I thought 'What is worthless singly, but worth having a million of?' Finally the idea of a million pennies struck and stuck."

So Rich fired up her principal; her husband who is a controller/treasurer at Coast Federal Bank; her community; parents throughout the school; local businessmen and even enlisted the local newspaper, *The Signal*, to issue a witty challenge to the Newhall Land and Farming Co. which eventually collected 300,000 pennies.

For over a year, they pinched and pulled together until they amassed 1 million pennies netting a cool $10,000. During the "Penny Project," Coast Federal stored the mountain of copper until they reached their goal. That's when they poured all the pennies on the cafeteria floor to get a true sense of what a million looks like.

Besides giving all the kids in the school a unique education on how to add, subtract, divide and multiply large numbers, the school purchased 8 new computers.

Could a bank, savings and loan or credit union in your hometown be so inclined to initiate a similar project to show children how to be penny wise and tons smarter?

(In 1998, Coast Federal merged with Home Savings of America.)

"Teacher Link"
1-On-1 Program Provides Missing Link For Computer-Shy Teachers

Often overlooked in the mad dash to bring computers into the K-12 classrooms are the current competencies and phobias of the K-12 teachers who are already overwhelmed as it is with the changing complexities of public education.

Only 1 in 5 nationwide teachers uses technology regularly to teach courses and most states report that training teachers to use computers in the classroom is their greatest need, according to the U.S. Department of Education.

Simplifying the tech stress of integrating computers is a model program called "Teacher Link" from Amdahl Corporation, a company that specializes in customizing computer solutions. **amdahl®**

Teacher Link works this way:

- A local school completes an Amdahl registration form.
- Amdahl next links a compatible corporate volunteer tutor with a single teacher.
- The tutor evaluates the school's current and future hardware and software.
- The tutor then outlines a customized plan that's in sync with the equipment and teacher's comfort level.

Sample 1-on-1 tutoring has included: Spreadsheets to track students' progress; school website design and Photoshop® for professionally-designed school newsletters, graphic materials and digital imaging.

For more information on this highly-effective model program, contact "Teacher Link," Corporate Affairs, Amdahl Corporation, 1250 East Arques Ave., Sunnyvale, CA 94088 or call 408-746-6000.

========

Simon & Schuster offers "Browser Basics for Teachers" and "Teaching with the Web" for professional development for K-12 teachers. **For more information, call 212-698-7000 or visit their website at http://www.edscape.com.**

BUSINESS #26

Florida Computer Consultants Plug In Have-Nots With Community Computer Recycling Program

Bridging the computer gap in our communities will be an ongoing dilemma well into the 21st Century.

But a couple computer consultants in Gainesville, FL have created a simple way to get "Have-Nots" up and clicking.

With over 150 clients and deep roots embedded in their community, Andrew Adkins and Joel Bridges not only knew how desperately churches, schools and social services needed new technology but also how their customers were regularly upgrading their computer equipment.

The trick was to connect the "Haves" with the "Have-Nots." According to *PC World*, here's how they did it:

- Established a Storage & Repair Station in an unused area of a school maintenance room.
- Contacted 35 computer dealers and consultants, 20 of whom served as drop-off points for old equipment.
- Got 12 volunteers to pick up and repair old computers from notices on the local Free-net and in user groups.
- Got volunteers to deliver and install the systems.

The results? An 18-year-old with cerebral palsy is able to communicate with a specially-equipped computer; a woman who opens her home to underprivileged youth received a computer and printer to help the kids with their homework and a Nigerian man is e-mailing to his hometown.

With 1000s of computer consultants spread across the U.S., it would only take a couple computer savants in every community to spearhead and execute this excellent and most adaptable computer recycling program.

"Ceramic Garden"
Clay Cafe Turns $10 Tiles Into $6000 Library Donation

You're a small, community-minded business …
And you need to expand or upgrade your store …
But you want to do it by helping a good cause.

Here's a clever way to refurbish while simultaneously replenishing a community resource.

Clay Cafe, a learn-on-the-urn pottery and ceramics studio in Calabasas, CA, wanted to transform a plant bed in front of their store into a "Ceramic Garden." Owners Marc and Clarice Gerstel collected sponsorships of $10 per tile with participants painting 4-inch squares to their individual whims such as "Calabasas Rules."

Approximately 650 tiles were painted and more than $6000 was donated to "Friends of the Calabasas Library" which then purchased CDs as well as children's library materials.

This business/community project worked well because of its low-cost-of-entry and a collective high return on investment as 100s of people reaped the rewards at the library.

Community good will and good business practices are stitched together by simple but permanent projects like this one. What sponsorships can you sell to draw attention to your business while helping your community?

For more information, contact Clay Cafe, 23653 Calabasas Rd., Calabasas, CA 91302 or call 818-591-7682.

Photo by Delmar Watson

Store Owner Makes Local Heroes Out Of Students By Giving Comic Books For A's

========

Begs The Question: Why Not a "Community Rewards Program?"

Action! Adventure! A's in English!

Cultivating youthful comic book customers who can also read is not a problem at Canyon Cards & Comics in Woodland Hills, CA.

The owners figured that instead of enticing new customers with coupons, they would put more substance into the promotion by offering free comic books for A's. That's why a sign in the front window reads: "Where There's An A, There's a Free Comic Book."

Every time an elementary or middle school student gets an A, he or she can receive a free comic book during a report card period.

What a smart and easy way to get students motivated to do well in school.

What if other businesses that cater to young people — fast-food restaurants, ice cream shops, movie theatres, skate and bicycle shops — all started a similar "Community Rewards Program" for students?

Kids would be trying harder in school (without parental nag) and collecting their favorite bounty all over town. It would be a very good thing.

BUSINESS #29

Industrial Designer Stirs The Luminescence Of Learning By Transforming New York Souls & Schools From The Inside Out

Proving that color — especially sassy, brassy color — is a catalyst for positive change in an austere and drab learning environment is industrial designer Ruth Lande Shuman who has become a galvanizing force transforming educational attitudes, attendance and test scores with coats of golden yellows, raspberry reds and rosy corals creatively painted over the walls, hallways, lockers and stairwells in a few of New York City's and New Jersey's grittiest public schools.

publi©olor

By all accounts, this is no cosmetic whitewash either.

"In general, the overall tone of the school has changed — there is a strong spirit of student ownership," wrote Lena Medley, principal at Thomas Jefferson High School in Brooklyn after one of Shuman's colorful makeovers. "I have been associated with Jefferson for over ten years, and as I write this, an amazing phenomenon has taken place — Jefferson is graffiti-free! Not a small accomplishment for this or any other public school!"

Through her volunteer-based, not-for-profit Publicolor organization, Shuman collects 500 gallons of donated Benjamin Moore paints; enlists corporate sponsors such as Bloomberg L.P. and Estee Lauder; organizes a Paint Club of committed students to create color schemes and designs and then rallies parents, teachers and sponsor employees to collaborate with the students who prime and paint each day after school and on Saturdays for 8-12 weeks.

"I try to stimulate the eye to help keep the mind alert," explained Shuman. In practice, her theory is working as a Bank Street College of Education study reports that Publicolor has been the primary reason behind a 15% increase in attendance, 15% improvement in math and reading scores and renewed student respect for their energized learning environment. Spillover effects include tapping new artistic talent, student-corporate networking and potential internships.

Publicolor supplies maintenance paint for 3 years as well as ongoing mentoring, leadership training and job preparedness programs to the students involved in the Paint Clubs.

For more information, contact Publicolor, 1120 Park Ave., Ste. 16C, New York, NY 10128 or call 212-722-2448.

CHAPTER 7

Portable Ideas For Small To Large Businesses

BUSINESS #30

"One to One/The National Mentoring Partnership"
Takes Mentoring Into Day-To-Day Reality With 61 Helpful Tools

Details, details.

While many of the 300 businesses at the 1997 President's Summit for America's Future in Philadelphia made commitments to start or increase mentoring programs (and reportedly 70% are making good on their pledges), the initial process for beginner businesses — from SOHO consultants to small firms to companies with 10,000 employees — may seem confusing for those who have the desire but don't know how to get started.

Well, a single call can do it all.

A virtual mentoring magnet, One to One/The National Mentoring

Partnership has evaluated step-by-step guides, manuals, videos, studies and research and compiled them into a list of 61 resources that collectively comprise the crucible of adult, teen or team mentoring.

THE NATIONAL MENTORING PARTNERSHIP

From recruiting volunteers to reaching the "hip-hop" generation, the National Mentoring Partnership has the tools to help motivate business owners to implement a customized, lasting and meaningful mentoring program for your company in your community.

Connecting a caring, empathetic adult to a vulnerable youth on a regular and committed schedule can become a synergistic series of defining moments that can propel the often at-risk student into superior academic achievement. In separate studies in Cincinnati and Chicago, 86% and 65% of the students with mentors, respectively, went on to college.

Working in partnership with Big Brothers Big Sisters of America, Harvard Center for Health Communications, The Points of Light Foundation, United Way and many others, the National Mentoring Partnership has a national goal of 2 million children being mentored by the year 2002.

To make it meaningful for a single business with 25, 250, 2500 or 25,000 employees, get a copy of "Select Mentoring Resources" by contacting One to One/The National Mentoring Partnership, 2801 M St., NW, Washington, DC, 20007 or calling 202-338-3844.

"Points of Light"
Makes Volunteerism a Core Function As Integral As Finance, Marketing, Personnel Or Sales

At the end of the 20th Century, American business is under unprecedented competition, rapid technological change, stickier government regulations and unbearable pressure to exceed the expectations of financial analysts.

Yet amidst this exigent coalescing of overwhelming management issues — combined with employees' daily fears of job security in an era of downsizing — a bright light has radiated into a few of America's top corporations.

"Business in the 1990s cannot operate as a unit separate from the rest of society," stated John Castle, board member of The Points of Light Foundation and an executive vice president at EDS. "To be effective, we must connect all parts of the community into a cohesive unit."

Founded in 1990; merged with the 500+ Volunteer Centers of the National Volunteer Center in 1991 and now working with 40 other national membership-based organizations through Connect America to get 10 million Americans to commit to service, Points of Light is energizing the volunteer movement to make it "a unit" or core function as integral as Finance, Marketing, Personnel or Sales.

To that end, the nonprofit, nonpartisan Points of Light Foundation is promoting "Volunteer Program Management" just like a company would market its products with a comprehensive assortment of books, audios, training manuals and videos.

Yet it is not an easy sell.

The well-known Points of Light Foundation lists only 162 corporate members on its 1997 roster. Where is the rest of corporate America? The fastest-growing *Inc.* 500? The *Fortune* 1000? The 25 million home businesses?

Although the documented research that directly links volunteering to profitability is moderate, companies that have extensive volunteer programs in the communities they serve are emanating a compelling and powerful light. They are finding they can attract and retain a more well-rounded and committed employee who has a higher level of teamwork, communication skills and dedication which are all values added into a company's product or service.

Despite that logical inter-connection, hopefully corporate volunteering won't follow a route similar to Total Quality Management (TQM).

In the 1980s, when U.S. companies tried to catch up with the quality of Japanese exports, CEOs made the egregious error of "delegating" the responsibility of transforming a company into a TQM organization.

Although poor quality was documented to show it can cost a company *as much as 25%* of sales, middle management and employees at most U.S. firms adopted a "malicious compliance" to quality circles, quality seminars and the entire quality movement. Since they didn't see the president or owner "walk the talk," they didn't truly accept it or make it work and subsequently TQM faded away.

Properly introduced as permanent policy by the CEO and then implemented and managed, employee volunteering *can become* a competitive edge in an ever more intense marketplace. Get your employees involved now and reap the dividends throughout the 21st Century.

For more information on how to incorporate volunteering into your strategic planning, contact Corporate Outreach and Services, The Points of Light Foundation, 1737 H St., NW, Washington, DC 20006 or call 202-223-9186.

"Business Coalition for Education Reform"
Gives Business Owners Vigorous Voice For Upgrading Education

Deep in the hills of Tennessee, business has gotten down into education.

What started out as a quiet request during job interviews at Eastman Chemical in Kingsport has galvanized the attention of students and parents and become a new hiring policy at *70 other employers* in northeast Tennessee and southwest Virginia.

The request? The job applicant is asked to submit a high school transcript of grades and attendance.

"No single act changed the face of education more," revealed Betty DeVinney, Eastman Chemical's manager of corporate relations which started its school performance record as a job criterion in 1989. Not only has the failure rate of entry-level employees hit an industry low but new employees are moving through apprenticeship programs with less need for remediation.

This is just one of the ideas a coalition at the National Alliance for Business is advocating for more entrepreneurs, business owners and corporate executives to adopt to strengthen America's public schools.

Making the overdue connection between public education and business, between complacency and competitiveness, between failure and success, a unique coalition of 13 national business organizations — including The Conference Board and National Association of Manufacturers among others — have forged nothing short of an allied force aimed at stemming the creeping erosion of a public education system that is sending too many 17- and-18-year-olds into the marketplace without fundamental or critical thinking skills needed to maintain a job. Called the Business Coalition for Education Reform (BCER), the group's primary focus is to raise educational standards to world-class levels in local school districts. To that end,

BCER offers an extensive "Standards Mean Business" compendium of resources including guides, kits, videos, books and other innovative materials to help business leaders better prepare youth as they enter the workforce in the 21st Century.

For a resource catalog, contact Business Coalition for Education Reform c/o National Alliance of Business, 1201 New York Ave., NW, Ste. 700, Washington, DC 20005; call 800-787-2848 or visit their website at http://www.bcer.org.

BUSINESS #33

"Share Our Strength"
Creates Business Model
For Cause-Related Marketing

Let's be honest. Corporate involvement with the 570,000 nonprofits in the U.S. is like watching a handful of beebees rolling around at the bottom of a barrel.

This lack of linkage has many reasons. One of the most prominent is management's prevailing belief that its *sole* social responsibility is the quarterly drum roll of ever-increasing profits.

A second reason is the prevailing absence of business sophistication at most nonprofits that undermines their passionate missions. This inability of nonprofits to operate like a business often inhibits many entrepreneurs, gazelles and small to large corporations from developing partnerships.

Creatively blending the private and nonprofit sectors in a mutually meaningful way in our New Economy is the innovative, well-managed and nonprofit Share Our Strength (SOS) which has crafted the art of business marketing to a nonprofit, also known as "cause-related marketing."

SHARE OUR STRENGTH

By skillfully using the familiar tools of marketing — benefits, events, sponsorships, licensing arrangements, cross-promotions, co-ventures and the basic sales of goods and services — SOS, which is completely independent of grants, foundations and government welfare, has distributed over $43 million to more than 1000 anti-hunger and anti-poverty organizations since its inception in 1984.

By mobilizing businesses of all sizes to contribute the products or talents of their respective industries, SOS most notably enlisted American Express to donate 3 cents from every card transaction over 60-day periods during their 4-year "Charge Against Hunger" campaign. Other alliances have been formed with Barnes & Noble, Calphalon, Evian, Fetzer Vineyards, E. & J. Gallo Winery and Restaurants Unlimited Inc. among others that collectively enable SOS to efficiently distribute 92.5% of its revenues to its many initiatives and causes.

To learn how to become a corporate partner with this successful nonprofit, contact Share Our Strength, 1511 K St., NW, Ste. 940, Washington, DC 20005; call 202-393-2925 or visit their website at http: //www.strength.org.

BUSINESS #34

"Business For Social Responsibility"
Blends 60s Idealism With 90s Networking

Do you want to grow your business and spread better business ethics at the same time?

Then consider the San Francisco-based Business For Social Responsibility (BSR). It's a group of more than 1400 nationwide companies from Taco Bell to Honeywell to Starbucks to start-ups to SOHO types and sole practitioners who practice a 1960s idealism within the realities of today's bottom-line business climate.

Basically, BSR promotes the 3 R's of business: Resources, Referrals and Responsibility.

By sharing resources and contacts, members of BSR can access copies of employee handbooks, child care policies, community involvement programs, its Corporate Social Responsibility "Starter Kit" and referrals to venture capitalists among many other socially responsible "best practices" and services. Although new members are not screened, BSR welcomes companies of all sizes.

By connecting among companies that have common human sensitivities, BSR members are not only doing well by doing good but also setting new standards of business ethics that can only better our local and global communities.

For information about becoming a member, contact Business For Social Responsibility, 609 Mission St., San Francisco, CA 94105; call 415-537-0888 or visit their website at http://www.bsr.org.

"INROADS"
Grooms Best & Brightest Minorities For Corporate & Community Service

For over 25 years, the St. Louis-based, nonprofit INROADS organization has paved the way for high-achieving minority students to get a foot in the front door of corporate America.

Through its 49 affiliate operations throughout the U.S., INROADS has over 6000 graduates who are pursuing professional and managerial careers.

With a goal of being the premiere supplier of minority talent, INROADS recruits students from local high schools and community groups; places them in paid summer internships and links them with employee mentors. Students must meet rigorous standards as only 80 interns were selected out of 1200 who applied during one application period in Southern California.

While the company pays a sponsorship fee and the interns' summer salary, it is still a cost-effective way to hire minority executives for global companies that want to stay competitive in a multicultural world. And it's paid off.

Over the past 5 years, 8 out of 10 graduates who received offers from their sponsors accepted full-time employment while 9 out of 10 sponsors recommended participation to other companies.

INROADS is looking for additional company sponsors seeking to make a commitment to minority youth.

For more information, contact INROADS, Inc., 10 South Broadway, Ste. 700, St. Louis, MO 63102 or call 314-241-7488.

Add Meaning To Corporate Meetings By Helping The Host Community

In lieu of holding a company golf tournament at your next meeting, why not take the collective energy of your employees and put them to work on a project in the host community?

That's what Kinko's did when 600 sales people met at the Wyndham Hotel in Palm Springs, CA for its annual meeting. After discussing their newest product, they then changed out of their suits and held their next meeting at a school.

Over 83% (500 out of 600) employees spent an afternoon painting the entire exterior surface to the run-down Cathedral Elementary School. Kinko's donated $5000 and more than 1000 hours of labor.

The school makeover became the highest-rated, team-building event in Kinko's history and, from now on, it will be done every year they meet in a different city.

========

A few other companies have done similar renovations in host communities. For example, GE Plastics refurbished 5 San Diego community facilities during a national meeting; employees at Hoechst Celanese Corporation often board buses at corporate conferences and dedicate afternoons at nonprofit organizations and 350 Novus employees (parent of Discover Card) spread 75 truckloads of mulch for a new playground in San Antonio during its annual card member conference.

BUT, in 1996, corporate America held more than *800,000 meetings* with more than 84 million employees attending.

What would it take to incorporate these-bonding-and-building projects into your corporate meetings in various host communities? The potential is exponential!

(©Kinko's, Inc. All depictions of Kinko's are the exclusive property of Kinko's, Inc. KINKO'S is a registered trademark of Kinko's Ventures, Inc. All depictions of Kinko's and its trademark are used by permission.)

"Gifts In Kind"
Lets You Donate Without Headache

Got the urge to give back to your community but don't have the time to get involved?

Then consider the wide range of "free donation management services" and tax benefits of giving new, excess or outdated products — typically clothing, computers, software or used furniture — to Gifts In Kind International.

GIFTS IN KIND INTERNATIONAL®

It, in turn, will direct your donation to registered 501(c)(3) charities serving the less fortunate in your local community, global community or to arts, environmental or cultural organizations.

Over 1000 companies have channeled their products into these charitable areas:

- Clothe & Comfort
- Emergency Relief
- Healthy from the Start
- Housing the Homeless
- Office Smart
- Recycle Technology
- Retail
- Transportation
- Youth Programs

For more information, contact Gifts In Kind International, 333 North Fairfax St., Alexandria, VA 22314; call 703-836-2121 or visit their website at http://www.GiftsInKind.org.

Wire a School To The Internet For $350

Pooling their electronic powers together is a savvy group of high-tech business volunteers who want to get all 140,000 U.S. schools wired to the Internet.

Ambitious, yes. Impossible, no.

Called "NetDay," the volunteer effort enables community-based businesses, entrepreneurs and unions to plug into your preferred school for an approximate $350 investment.

Here's how to be a NetDay Sponsor:

- Go to the home page at … **http://www.netday.org** and click to the "NetDay School Search Form." Or call the principal and let the school know you want to sponsor a NetDay Kit.
- When your school chooses a Kit, it contacts you with details on how to place the order.

The task to electronically upgrade our public schools is daunting. While the federal E-rate that provides generous discounts through a $2.25 billion fund will help considerably, other issues must be addressed. As *The Wall Street Journal* has reported "… in most of the nation's schools, few teachers have yet integrated the Internet into their lesson plans. The hurdles are towering — and go well beyond the nuts-and-bolts of hard-wiring."

While lack of teacher training; difficulty of putting phone lines into schools and academic concerns about emphasizing the Internet over the fundamental subjects of math, English and basic critical thinking skills are drawbacks, NetDay is nevertheless a worthy endeavor and one that more businesses should join to make the next generation the savvy electronic powerhouse of the 21st Century.

"Youth Enrichment Foundation"
Salt Lake City Businessman Bolsters Art & Music Programs

In 1993, Jim Cox took stock of 3 developments:

- Art, music and other enrichment programs were being eliminated in public schools.
- He knew these programs can have profound impacts on students' academic abilities, self-esteem and personal development. (For example, the Duke Ellington School in Washington, DC has one of the lowest dropout rates in the nation while 90% of the participants in The Boys Choir of Harlem go on to college.)
- Check-writing for good causes left him skeptical of its effectiveness.

After conducting further research, Cox learned he could form an "operating foundation" whereby he and other business donors could *specifically* select the elementary school and programs they wanted to sponsor; be guaranteed that 100% of their money would be used at that school and receive regular progress reports on their donation.

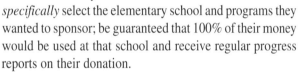

It all added up to creating the "Youth Enrichment Foundation" (YEF), a customized, hands-on philanthropic organization.

With a full-time staff including teachers, administrators and volunteers, the YEF chose a local elementary school and purchased 135 piano keyboards as well as art supplies.

"Children who have traditionally struggled with 'the basics' are now feeling a sense of pride and accomplishment as they display their beautiful works of art or are applauded after performing in a mini-elementary recital," reported Patti O'Keefe, principal at Whittier Elementary in Salt Lake City. "We firmly believe that success breeds success — students who can see improvements in their keyboarding skills can transfer that sense of accomplishment to other areas of the curriculum."

With sufficient resources in the General Administration Fund to run the current programs for 8 years, the YEF also has commitments of over $500,000 per year for the next several years to provide for additional schools.

What would it take to initiate a similar foundation in your local school district?

To find out how enriching it can be, contact the Youth Enrichment Foundation, P.O. Box 581049, Salt Lake City, UT 84158 or call 801-978-8016 or 801-481-4846.

"Business Watch"
Tire Dealer Straightens Up a Community

Like many frustrated small businessmen throughout the U.S., tire dealer Flip Smith in Van Nuys, CA watched in dismay as his main street turned

into seedy street via the splotchy arrival of crime, grime and the slime of prostitution.

But unlike other businessmen, he found the time to be a mobilizing force of one by starting a "Business Watch."

From a sparse first meeting of 13 fellow businessmen in December, 1992, Smith's "Business Watch" has mushroomed to 420 receiving his newsletter with about 50-60 regularly attending his monthly meetings.

The bottom line along a 6-mile corridor?

"The street's clean; there's no graffiti anywhere; there are no abandoned cars; curbsides are better; every apartment building is looking good and prostitution is just about gone," he proudly stated.

Winner of the 1997 Small Business Advocate for the state of California, Smith publishes an action-oriented newsletter that's jammed with success stories and phone numbers.

Topics have included:

• Abandoned Vehicles
• Cellular Phone Theft
• "Hot Lines" for Arson, Drugs & Fraud
• Scam Alerts

"If you want to start a Business Watch in your community, look around and see what your concerns are," he advised. "Every community will be different. Also, use the Senior Lead Officer at your community's police station because every time you bring a policeman with his local crime trends and his gun, it's a common draw to get business people out and get them motivated."

For information on how to start your own "Business Watch," contact Flip Smith, Flip's Tire Center, 7735 Sepulveda Blvd., Van Nuys, CA 91405 or call 818-786-8686.

"Community Scholarship Circle"
Education Grants For Students Who Live Within a 5-Mile Radius Of Your Business

An inventive way to give back to your community is by establishing an educational incentive for the sons and daughters of your closest customers or clients.

Whether you're an entrepreneur; run a small retail or mid-size to large business, you can organize a "Community Scholarship Circle."

Since 1973, the Lakewood (CA) Medical Center Foundation Pharmacy — a nonprofit arm of the Lakewood Regional Medical Center — has donated more than $1 million in scholarships to students who live within a 5-mile radius of the pharmacy.

To be eligible, students must live within the designated area; plan to attend medical, nursing or pharmaceutical school and "are judged on financial need, character, achievement, and a willingness to give back to the community," according to the *Press-Telegram*.

To reinvest in your repeat customers who regularly reinvest in you, this Community Scholarship Circle could be an excellent way to show your appreciation for the short-term and continue strengthening your long-term position by enabling local students to pursue careers in your industry.

For more information, contact the Lakewood Medical Center Foundation, 3650 South St., Ste. 100, Lakewood, CA 90712 or call 562-633-1150.

"STAR" & "COMET"
Enrichment Programs
Send At-Risk Students Soaring

Instead of watching students slide from one foster home to the next, a comprehensive school enrichment program is helping these same students graduate from grade to grade and on to college.

With the notion that caring is as much a part of a school curriculum as algebra and computers, the Institute for Community Development (ICD) in Manhasset, NY has developed 2 exemplary programs with a 96% success rate "through a unique, caring, holistic methodology of comprehensive, long-term academic enrichment, counseling and personal development."

Targeting at-risk students in the economically depressed minority school districts of Bedford Stuyvesant/Fort Green in Brooklyn; Roosevelt, Hempstead and Wyandanch on Long Island; Mt. Vernon and Troy, NY, the COMET program identifies at-risk 7th and 8th graders while the STAR program embraces 9th graders all the way through graduation.

From the first 3 STAR groups in 1994, 1995 and 1996, all of the students have received their high school diplomas. Even more impressive is that 96% of these students have gone to college with most of them being the first in their families.

There are now 1300 students in the combined programs and ICD is developing new partnerships annually.

Created by Gerard and Lilo Leeds, founders of CMP Media Inc., ICD has students and their parents sign a "contract" that they will participate in a slate of academic enrichment programs, counseling and career planning for at least 2 hours a day before, during and after school. At a cost of $3000 to $5000 per year per student, the programs are seeded by aggressive fundraising in corporate, foundation and philanthropic communities and by state education funds.

The 4-year, $20,000 investment reaps huge dividends considering that society gains approximately $500,000 from a lifetime of tax payments combined with the elimination of criminal justice and welfare costs.

For information on how these programs could be implemented by a caring company, contact the Institute for Community Development, 600 Community Dr., Manhasset, NY 11030 or call 800-891-3046.

"$2 Phone Home Cards"
Creative Local Fundraiser
For Community Children

'Why didn't you call?' is a question every worried parent has asked his or her child at one time or another.

'I didn't have any money,' is a familiar kid response.

Well an entrepreneur from Ventura, CA believes that conversation should never take place.

"We know that if you give a child $2 in cash, chances are they will spend it on candy or video games," explained entrepreneur Bob Brill. "But if they have a plastic phone card in their wallet or purse, parents can be sure their children will have the means to 'phone home' in an emergency."

At the LAPD Community Service and Youth Activity Center, Brill donated nearly $1000 in phone card time to the dozens of children who visit the afterschool facility. He suggests that other community-minded businesses could purchase bundles of these phone cards and give them to schools to use as fundraisers instead of selling candy bars and boxes of cookies.

"I hope others will follow along with what I've done in helping to add to child security ..." added Brill.

For more information on how your company could start a Phone Home Card fundraiser, contact Brill Productions, Inc. P.O. Box 7408, Ventura, CA 93006 or call 805-658-1076.

Pull Some Strings
For an Orphanage

Consider the 100s of orphanages in the U.S. that could use a helping hand.

Now consider it only takes one human torch to light the fire of hope and renewal in the eyes of 1000s of emotionally troubled children who are living in these facilities.

Inspired by the "Make a Difference Day" campaign, Dave Waterbury, a musician who lives in Van Nuys, CA, pulled all the strings for a humongous party for the 120 children at the Hathaway Children's Services orphanage in nearby Sylmar.

"I learned — as cliché as it might sound — one person can make a difference in the world, and I proved it to myself. I didn't really believe it was true," he admitted in the *Daily News*. "I wanted to help kids because they have their whole life ahead of them and maybe they will remember this and do something for someone in the future, if nothing else, maybe lighten their load of sadness."

Included in Waterbury's day of planned activities were a clown, a magician, an actress who played Pocahontas, Frisbees, blue jeans, wristwatches, baseball caps, T-shirts, books, games and trophies. Waterbury, who had never done anything like this before, recalled, "It was all worth it."

What would it take to for another musician, a consultant, a home-based business or a sole practitioner to plan a day like Waterbury's for an orphanage in your community?

It could be a day that could change a kid. For life!

For more information about Waterbury's Day, contact Hathaway Children's Services, P.O. Box 923670, Sylmar, CA 91392 or call 818-896-2474.

"2-Tier Mini-Grants"
REI Seeds Grass Roots Nonprofits

Is your company or business looking for a new and creative approach to philanthropy?

Then consider the model program established by Recreational Equipment Inc., better known as REI.

REI wants the environment to last just like the rugged equipment it sells.

So, since 1976, the nation's largest consumer cooperative has donated over $5 million in grants to 100s of mostly grass roots nonprofits. Its "2-tier" approach gives grants to worthy nonprofit groups which either ...

- Promote long-range **Conservation** of public lands, lakes and rivers or ...
- Stimulate **Community Recreation** opportunities.

Grants to Conservation groups average $3000 while Community Recreation groups receive grants averaging $250 to $1000.

In 1996, recipients included the American Hiking Society ($10,000); California Wilderness Coalition ($2968); Georgia Forest Watch ($4000); New York-New Jersey Trail Conference ($15,000) and the Wyoming Outdoor Council ($2500) among many others. For the year, over $418,000 was donated to Conservation groups and over $139,000 to Community Recreation organizations.

While grant applications are fairly streamlined, REI has very specific, locally-based, measurable guidelines that must be met to receive a grant.

This creative philanthropical structure could easily be adapted by other companies seeking ways to give back to their communities.

For more information on this common sense approach, contact REI, P.O. Box 1938, Sumner, WA 98390 or call its grants hotline at 206-395-7100.

Florist Hands Out 1200 Roses
To People Who Make "Sidewalk Pledge"

Trying to find a way to revitalize a sense of community in the San Fernando Valley suburb of Chatsworth, CA, florist Jay Berger had a bright idea one gloomy day in September, 1995.

What if he gave away a dozen roses to anyone who would first (a) take his "Sidewalk Pledge" to be a good neighbor and then as a Pledgee (b) would promise to give away the remaining 11 roses to strangers as a way of spreading his good neighbor policy?

Corny? You bet. But it worked!

Over 100 people took the pledge (twice what he predicted) and 1200 roses were distributed.

One woman spread the flowers around a Chatsworth convalescent home while another said she wanted to surprise parents at a nearby middle school.

Well maybe they fudged a little on the promise to give them to strangers but the message of spreading unexpected joy via the beauty of roses was carried out.

Small businesses do not necessarily have small ideas when it comes to putting a sense of quality into the community.

Think of the possibilities of creating your own Sidewalk Pledge in your hometown.

Unocal Gives Used Computers To Inmates Who Refurbish Them For Schools

Talk about your successful recycling program. This one moves to the top of the bin. Here's how it worked:

- Don Gluyas, an operations manager at Unocal, read a letter-to-the-editor in his local *Ventura County Star* (CA) about the need for old computers at the Todd Road Jail Computer Shop. So he called and donated 386 PCs (14 in all), 14 keyboards and 5 monitors.
- The inmates tinkered them into 10 usable systems.
- Once retrofitted, the computers were delivered to the nearby San Cayetano School in Fillmore.

UNOCAL 76 "We've given away $10,000 and $20,000 before with not much of an appreciative response from other groups," said Gluyas from his office in Ventura. "But after those kids got their computers, did we ever get some heartfelt letters. It sure beat giving away money; it was something special."

Do you have surplus computers at your company or do you know a company that does? Do you know a school that's badly in need of computers? If so, then you can initiate a similar computer/human recycling program in your hometown.

There are at least 3 organizations that can help facilitate the process:

- East West Education Development Foundation sends working computer components to nonprofit organizations in the U.S. and abroad. **Call 617-261-6699.**

- The Detwiler Foundation Computers for Schools Program was instrumental in arranging Unocal's computers-to-jail- to-schools project. Designated for California schools only, the program stipulates that donated computer hardware must at least be a 486. **Call 800-939-6000 or visit their website at http://www.detwiler.org**.

- The National Cristina Foundation connects companies and individuals who want to donate to groups that train people with disabilities or economic disadvantages. **Call 800-274-7846.**

PART III

Schools   K-12

Here are 49 innovative, in-place projects, programs or ideas for direct implementation into your hometown schools.

They were selected for their:

- Creativity;

- General ease of adaptability throughout the U.S.;

- Potential long-term impact on the quality of the entire school district;

- Ability to be initiated by a single parent, student, concerned citizen, teacher or school administrator with a phone, pen or Internet access;

- Ability to create "outside the box" learning projects; bring an infusion of resources; address racism; stimulate critical thinking skills; implement creative ways to include parents in the educational process; strengthen greater environmental awareness; provide contacts of outside organizations to initiate reform; accelerate Internet connections into the classroom; enable teachers to get electronically up to speed; deter crime; instill character; foster safety; develop intergenerational empathy and understanding; widen the role of schools into full-time community centers; enhance physical appearance of facilities and playgrounds; motivate community professionals to become more active partners and generally inspire teachers, students and parents by raising their collective spirit.

CHAPTER 8

Pre-School

Schools K-12

"Parents as Teachers"
Education Program Begins On Way Home From Hospital; Scores an Early "A"

Capitalizing on how babies start learning within days of birth and how they can hear and remember words as young as 8 months old, a home-school-community partnership program called "Parents as Teachers" has earned a remarkable success record since its inception in 1981.

Encouraging parents, including teenage parents, to see themselves as their "child's first and most influential teacher," Parents as Teachers is a voluntary program that teaches parents child development from birth to age 5.

Personalized home visits by some 8000 certified parent educators are helping parents understand what to expect in each stage of their child's development. They also offer tips on how to encourage learning, e.g.

"tummy time" to let babies explore a colorful cardboard box; how to manage challenging behavior and promote strong parent-child relationships.

Child graduates have performed significantly higher than national norms on measures of intellectual and language abilities. Also, developmental delays were resolved for half of identified children by age 3.

There are now over 1900 Parents as Teachers program sites in 47 states and 6 countries. This program not only strengthens the crucial importance of the parent's role in education but also stimulates parental participation throughout a child's school year. That continual intervention would help teachers immensely as a survey by the National Education Association found that more than 90% of teachers want

more parental involvement. In fact, "parental indifference" often rates *above* low salaries as a cause of dissatisfaction with our nation's teachers.

For information on the site closest to you or how to start a program, contact Parents as Teachers National Center, Inc., 10176 Corporate Square Dr., Ste. 230, St. Louis, MO 63132; call 314-432-4330 or visit their website at http://www.patnc.org.

========

A smaller, single year, pre-school program — known as "Success By 6" — was started in 1989 by the United Way. Over 200 communities now have coalitions of public, private and philanthropic resources running pre-schools that are designed specifically for 4-year-olds.

For more information, contact the United Way of America at 800-892-2757, ext. 516.

Give Pre-schoolers "The Marshmallow Test" To Teach Delayed Gratification

Teach delayed gratification early and you'll enhance a child for life.

During the 1960s, an obscure "Marshmallow Test" was performed on a group of pre-school kids on the campus of Stanford University. The teacher said they had 2 choices:

(A) If they could wait until he returned from a 20-minute errand, they could have 2 marshmallows. Or …

(B) If they could *not* wait until his return, they could have *1* marshmallow right away, but only one.

The results:

- Some 12 to 14 years later, the kids who waited were better able to cope with the frustrations of life; embraced challenges; were self-reliant; took initiative; were dependable and trustworthy. The kids who immediately grabbed the marshmallow were easily upset by frustration; resentful of others; immobilized by stress; saw themselves as bad or unworthy; got into fights and overreacted to irritation with a sharp temper.

- The most dramatic follow-up was on SAT scores. The kids who waited had test results that were *210 points higher* on their SATs than the 4-year-olds who could not delay gratification.

"At age four, how children do on this test of delay of gratification is twice as powerful a predictor of what their SAT scores will be as is IQ at age four," wrote Daniel Goleman who reported this phenomenon in his landmark book, *Emotional Intelligence.*

Is there a way to make "The Marshmallow Test" a learning experience in every pre-school, kindergarten and first grade throughout the U.S?

The "test" should not only be conducted but also examples and projects should be made a part of every curriculum — with explanations sent home to parents so they can add to the learning process — to implant this lifelong social skill.

CHAPTER 9

Innovative Learning

Schools K-12

George Lucas Becomes "Yoda For Public Education" With Epochal Navigational Guide For Price Of Only 3 Matinees

George Lucas of "Star Wars" infamy has created another work of epochal proportions. But this one isn't for sci-fi fans.

This production is for anyone who cares about the real life consequences and baseline urgency to reinvent, restore and re-energize public education as the primary force that must be with us as we enter the 21st Century.

"I believe public education is the cornerstone of our society," wrote George Lucas in the opening to his 300-page, call-to-action book titled *Learn & Live* that lists scores of innovative efforts already in place and 100s of resources to trigger an avalanche of new thinking and new ways of teaching.

"It is the foundation of our freedom and a vital building block of our democracy — a stepping stone for young and old alike to reach their full potential. And that's why people are so passionate about it. The challenge we face today is to translate this passion into action and reinvigorate public education. If we are successful, we can make a vast difference in the quality of life for our children, ourselves, and for future generations."

Divided into 4 relevant categories — Students, Teachers, Communities and Schools — the education-friendly book is a masterful navigational blueprint for steering innovative teaching and learning into the forefront of everyone's responsibility.

Here are just a few of the innovative projects and programs:

- Critique Circles
- Foxfire Approach
- Graduation by Exhibition
- MicroSociety Schools
- Portfolio Audits
- Teaching Externships

A 1-hour documentary illustrates some of the creative technologies and is a visual companion to this book that should be required reading by every school teacher and every member of every school board in the U.S. today!

For more information about this $20 bargain package, contact George Lucas Educational Foundation, P.O. Box 672, Santa Rosa, CA 95402; call 888-4RKIDS1 or visit their website at http://glef. org.

"Telementoring"
Links 2000 Hewlett-Packard Employees To 1000 Students & 300 Teachers

In lieu of employees leaving their jobs to mentor students, Hewlett-Packard (HP) conducts a savvy "Telementoring" program that creates 1-to-1 mentoring relationships among HP employees worldwide with 5th to 12th grade students and their teachers throughout the U.S.

"Alex Kopperud of Palmer, Alaska and I matched up in a telementoring relationship on January 21, 1997," explained David Neils, HP's Mentor Program Manager in Ft. Collins, CO.

"We worked together on a website where he can receive feedback on his photographs from successful outdoor photographers from around the world. In addition to helping students excel in math and science, telementoring is an excellent tool to help students chart a successful path to pursue a dream like outdoor photography."

HP's non-commercial Telementoring website is intelligently organized as it clearly explains how teachers can register their students with an HP mentor; see sample lesson plans and projects and join online discussion groups with fellow teachers.

Initiated in 1995, HP's Telementoring program shows how an industry leader is setting an electronic example for strengthening our educational system by linking caring and committed volunteer employees to mentor students online. It's the next best thing to being there!

To complete an online application for HP mentoring for your students, visit their website at http://mentor.external.hp.com.

"C-CAP"
Redefines "Home Ec" Into "Culinary Arts"
Students Eat Their Homework, Then Go To Work

High school Home Economics is no longer a "cake" course, thanks to the nonprofit Careers Through Culinary Arts Program or C-CAP.

Very simply, C-CAP is one of the most innovative upgrades to the classroom in the 1990s. By transforming the teaching of home economics into the meaningful application of food preparation, a whole new generation of gourmet grads has headed straight into the kitchens of haute cuisine restaurants hungry for their hip talent and honest enthusiasm.

While the NBA plucks high school players like Kobe Bryant off the court with the hope of becoming the next Michael Jordan, C-CAP gives students a more realistic life direction with a truer hope of becoming the next Wolfgang Puck.

Since 1990, over 10,000 students in 9 metropolitan school districts have completed the comprehensive C-CAP courses. Many of these students are now employed in the foodservice industry.

By bringing together local corporate sponsors, chefs-as-mentors and other professionals, teachers are elevating their lesson plans with a well-conceived soufflé of 4 years of culinary tools to greatly enhance their curricula while simultaneously bubbling up renewed passion for their teaching profession.

Besides earning $3.2 million in scholarships to prestigious culinary schools, students can also achieve apprenticeships and internships that C-CAP organizes with local restaurants, hotels and hospitality establishments.

This public-private, school-to-work program is a national model for other industries — such as fashion design, graphic arts and auto repair — to create similar professional training infrastructures in public schools.

For more information on how to start C-CAP in your school, contact Careers Through Culinary Arts Program, Inc., 155 West 68th Street, New York, NY 10023 or call 212-873-2434.

"Future Problem Solving Program"
Is a No-Brainer; Make It Mandatory In Every School!

Considering the usually metronomic rhythms of public education, an intelligent course of thought — that compels students to research, *think* and creatively make decisions about future problems — has such utter common sense it's inconceivable (even though it was introduced in 1974) it's not a mandatory program in every school.

But don't take my recommendation.

"If you're an adult who has wondered whether it was possible to get kids to *think*, to be creative and analytical when it comes to complex social issues, you can relax," observed Kathy O'Malley in the *Chicago Tribune*. "With Future Problem Solvers, it's already being done."

The "Future Problem Solving Program" (FPSP) consists of 4 students on a team and a teacher/coach who guides them through 6 steps:

- Identify topic-related challenges
- Identify an underlying problem
- Generate potential solutions
- Generate criteria to judge solutions
- Evaluate solutions to determine the best one
- Develop action plan

Challenging students to think through complex issues, the program addresses 3 problem areas during the school year. The students then write and mail possible solutions to an FPSP evaluator for feedback. Student-Teams which are competing with other schools range from grades 4-12. (In the non-competitive component, FPSP is available for grades K-12.)

Two of its headline successes include an FPSP team in Massachusetts that designed a waste water plant building and saved their community $120,000 while another team raised funds to restore the battleship *Texas*.

To bring this most progressive program to your school, contact Illinois-FPSP, Inc., 1320 Anderson Dr., Ste. 1000, Batavia, IL 60510 or call 800-544-3772.

Schools #7

"Kids on the Block"

Puppet Troupe Creates Moments Of Truth Transcending Into Empathy

One of the passionate joys of teaching is seeing that flash of understanding light up a child.

And one of the knotty areas of teaching is the awkwardness of topics that are often too touchy to address, especially in this era of excessive political correctness.

The Kids on the Block

However there is an engaging ensemble of kid-sized puppets — known as "Kids on the Block" — that cleverly clarifies the confusion and misperceptions that swirl around the developing minds of children and creates flashes of understanding in those sometimes unapproachable areas.

By using colorful props, well-researched information, humorous scripts, music and Q&A time, the hip racially-balanced puppet troupe can put on a customized assembly performance that creates moments of honest and free expression that suspend normal hesitation about sensitive topics.

Since its inception, Kids on the Block has developed a wide variety of educational curricula. Programs on disability/inclusion issues, medical or educational differences and social concerns are supplemented with follow-up materials, discussion and classroom activities. A "how to" video helps prepare puppeteers for their first performance. In lieu of teachers taking on the responsibility of putting on the show, many schools have volunteer puppeteers from community service organizations who love to perform. Either way, Kids on the Block can teach everlasting empathy by having charismatic characters reach deep within a child.

For more information, contact The Kids on the Block, Inc., 9385-C Gerwig Lane, Columbia, MD 21046; call 800-368-KIDS; or visit their website at http://www.kotb.com.

"ARTS Partners"
Establishes Culture Crusade In Grades 2-8

- 6th graders attend a Houston Symphony concert and learn how computers are used in music.

- 7th graders visit Houston's Museum of Fine Arts; discover what choices artists make and then create their own visual arts project in the classroom.

- 8th graders attend an Alley Theatre performance of "A Christmas Carol" and then calculate what Bob Cratchit's salary would be in today's economy.

Transforming the school art experience from a single year-end "field trip" to a year-round, student-centered, comprehensive community collaboration designed to integrate culture trips with in-school performances, artists-in-classrooms and relevant project assignments, "ARTS Partners" is a model program that is increasing academic achievement and enriching the lives of students in a culturally and economically diverse school district.

Comprised of 18,000 students in a suburb of Houston, the Spring Branch Independent School District uses a truly unique collaboration of resources including corporate sponsors, major arts organizations, school personnel and hometown volunteers.

And it's paying off.

By emphasizing cross-cultural experiences through the arts, all ethnic groups in the school district are scoring an average of *10% higher* on the Texas Assessment of Academic Skills in math, writing and reading than state averages. SAT scores in Spring Branch are also the highest in the Houston area and well above county, state and national averages.

For more information on this award-winning culture crusade, contact "ARTS Partners," Spring Branch Independent School District, P.O. Box 19432, Houston, TX 77224 or call 713-464-1511.

"CityWORKS"
Plants Seeds — Weeds Out Cynicism

Some teenage students can be cynical when they talk about their hometowns.

But in Cambridge, MA, they develop ideas for community redevelopment.

A novel 9th grade course — known as "CityWORKS" — at the Rindge School of Technical Arts checks all that sassiness at the classroom door. Armed with cameras, camcorders and notepads, they get under the skin of what makes their city tick and learn first-hand about diversity, landmarks, city resources and city opportunities. Then they decide what might make the community more useful and plan redevelopment projects such as a Discovery Museum, an auto body shop and a teen activities center among others. Once they decide on a project, they make blueprints and models for viewing at an Open House.

CityWORKS

Other aspects of the course include the Egg Crush Project, CityWORKS Resumé, City Shapes and Teammate Interviews among others.

Initial inspiration for the unique course came from the "Walk Around the Block" curriculum developed by The Center For Understanding the Built Environment.

For more information about adapting this community building curriculum, contact the Rindge School of Technical Arts, 459 Broadway, Cambridge, MA 02139 or call 617-349-6767.

SCHOOLS #10

"Exploratorium"
Takes Mustiness Out Of Museums & Science

Sparking students in the wonder of science, art and human perception is an increasingly difficult assignment for today's teachers.

When you're competing against CDs, Sega and the latest Tyrannosaurus from Spielberg, it is not easy for middle and high school science and math teachers to come up with competing special effects in the classroom.

A leap in that direction, however, is The Exploratorium Teacher Institute — a 4-week summer workshop — that gives teachers a learn-by-doing, inquiry-based approach to their profession.

It includes interactive museum exhibits, hands-on activities for classrooms back home and small group discussions of science content and pedagogy. All workshops begin with a study of perception and branch out into the topic areas.

Participants cover various subjects including physical science, life science, integrated science, general science, chemistry, math, English as a Second Language and special education.

Founded in 1969 by physicist and educator Frank Oppenheimer, the Exploratorium has become an internationally-acclaimed science center.

For more information about this science summer camp for teachers, contact The Exploratorium Teacher Institute, 3601 Lyon St., San Francisco, CA 94123; call 415-561-0313 or visit their website at http://www.exploratorium.edu.

"YES! Tour"
Makes Earth Come Alive With Green Teens

An assembly program that educates and entertains teens about the environment. What could be more natural?

A power-packed, 45-60 minute, multimedia show using humor, slides, live music and young presenters is making science textbooks come to life. Over 500,000 students have been stimulated by the touring "**Y**outh for **E**nvironmental **S**anity" (YES!) school assemblies.

 YOUTH FOR ENVIRONMENTAL SANITY

Always underscored with a hopeful message, the YES! presentation can be customized to 10 different themes:

- Air, Water & Land Pollution
- Apathy & Carelessness
- Environmental Racism
- Global Warming & Climate Change
- Green Schools Energy Project
- Healthy Schools Lunch Program
- Ozone Layer Depletion
- Recycling
- Saving our Forests
- Starting an Environmental Club

Following each YES! presentation is a "PowerHour" for up to 50 students. Questions are answered and opportunities and solutions provided.

Then, after a week of assemblies throughout the school district, the YES! tour concludes with a 1-day workshop.

For more information about making a date with this environmental ensemble, contact Youth For Environmental Sanity, 706 Frederick St., Santa Cruz, CA 95062, call 408-459-9344 or visit their website at http://www.yesworld.org.

"Nature's Web"
Weaves Environmental Lesson Plans Seemlessly Into The 21st Century

While "strategic planning" is well known in the business world, it is absolutely, overwhelmingly refreshing to see a group like the National Wildlife Federation present a 5-year strategic plan for teaching environmental education for students K-8 through the year 2001.

The template driving the lesson plan is simply called "Nature's Web."

In their own words, "we invite you (teachers) to see the interconnected wholeness of nature — which is to see more than the separate parts. Even as individual silk strands under various dynamic tensions comprise a complete orb web, so do the many aspects of nature we study comprise an integrated whole. This is nature's web — even more a wonder of beauty and genius than a spider's web.

NATIONAL WILDLIFE FEDERATION®

"Given the richness of the theme, plans are underway to expand it into a series of subthemes over the years 1997-2001, each of which will have its own particular educational goals."

Through a series of 10 lesson plans, Nature's Web thoughtfully presents easy-to-follow curriculum concepts illustrated with colorful posters and creative resource suggestions such as how your school can become a certified "Schoolyard Habitat."

Not only are most of the materials provided for free but the National Wildlife Federation openly seeks input from teachers on how to continuously improve their materials in addition to offering teachers a chance to win a trip to the Federation's annual Conservation Summit.

For more information, contact National Wildlife Federation, 8925 Leesburg Pike, Vienna, VA 22184; call 800-822-9919 or visit their website at http://www.nwf.org.

"Audubon Adventures"
Teaches Stewardship For Nature For Only $35 a Year

By emphasizing "inquiry as a way of achieving knowledge," the National Audubon Society offers a creative compendium of teaching tools that artfully present scientifically-based introductions to birds, wildlife and habitats and how their integrated cycles must be protected to preserve the delicate balance of man and nature.

National Audubon Society

Called "Audubon Adventures," the packet of year-long materials contains:

- 5 newspapers with last one keyed to Earth Day
- 72-page Teacher's Resource Manual
- 20-minute video
- Toll-free support line

Geared primarily for grades 4-6, it only costs $35 for a class of 32 students.

Incorporating drawings, charts, stories, short and long-term environmental changes in habitats as well as the study of migrations, this collective set is updated every year. It encourages students to test their own theories against scientific knowledge and then share their findings with local and global communities. Cost of these packets is often subsidized by local Audubon chapters.

To enhance students' appreciation of the stewardship for nature, contact Educational Division, National Audubon Society, 700 Broadway, New York, NY 10003 or call 800-813-5037.

"ONE IN A MILLION"
Campaign Has Students Rooting For The Future

Teachers and schools looking for a meaningful millennium project that plants the seeds of environmentalism as well as self-esteem should consider joining the ONE IN A MILLION Campaign.

The goal: Get young people rooting for the future by planting 1 million trees by the year 2000.

A collaborative effort between the El Segundo, CA-based Tree

Musketeers and the Nashville, TN-based Kids For A Clean Environment, this spirited campaign is a concerted effort that also easily teaches young people they too can make a difference, especially if you are one in this million.

By planting a tree in their backyard — or even in some community location — students can also develop the parallel growth of their own self-esteem as the tree matures with them over the years.

Plus they'll have the added joy of giving back to the environment as they learn about the multiple benefits of trees. Simultaneously, they:

- Absorb carbon dioxide
- Add 7% to 20% to a home's value
- Provide fruits, nuts, shade and habitats
- Reduce air conditioning bills 10% to 50%
- Stimulate oxygen
- Ventilate the planet

For more information on how to get students "rooting" for the future, contact ONE IN A MILLION Campaign, P.O. Box 158254, Nashville, TN 37215 or call 800-473-0263.

"Adopt-a-Raptor"
In Alaska And Diffuse
The Nightmarish Myths Of Movies

With most students' understanding of "raptors" coming from "Jurassic Park" and its nightmarish ability to scare the beeswax out of kids, the "Adopt-a-Raptor" program in Alaska allows students all across the lower 49 states to care and nurture for these precious, borderline endangered and always awesome birds to impart some reality into the myth-making.

For example, "Twinky," a female bald eagle who has a permanently-damaged wingtip from a gunshot wound, is up for adoption. Other eagles, hawks, falcons, owls and corvids (ravens) with similar injuries are also available for classroom adoption at the Alaska Raptor Rehabilitation Center (ARRC) in Sitka, AK.

Classroom sponsors receive:

- Adoption certificate
- ARRC video
- Curriculum packet
- 1-year ARRC membership
- Photo & Biography of "Twinky"
- Quarterly newsletter

This innovative program teaches students how to care long-distance; imparts real-life geography lessons about our nation's largest state; mitigates students' fears and even has opportunities to volunteer during the summer.

Cost of the classroom adoption is $75, a bargain considering the multiple learning experiences it can deliver.

For more information, contact Alaska Raptor Rehabilitation Center, 1101 Sawmill Creek Rd., P.O. Box 2984, Sitka, AK 99835; call 907-747-8662 or visit their website at http://www.halcyon.com/jeanluc/ ARRC/A.R.R.C.html.

========

While some zoos also have adoption programs, here are 2 other groups which facilitate bird adoptions: **Contact HawkWatch International, P.O. Box 660, Salt Lake City, UT 84110 (801-524-8520) or Rocky Mountain Raptor Program, Colorado State University, 300 West Drake, Ft. Collins, CO 80523 (970-491-0398).**

"Wildlife On Wheels"
A Live Interactive Roadshow In The Classroom

Animals and children have always been natural bonding agents outside the classroom.

Now a nonprofit organization dedicated to wildlife conservation through education can bring a Moluccan Cockatoo and his many friends inside the classroom.

WILDLIFE ON WHEELS

Based in Sunland, CA, "Wildlife On Wheels" (WOW) offers a 5-week series of classroom visits hosted by wildlife instructors. Not just show-and-tell sessions, these 40-minute classes stimulate students to see animals and ecosystems as major role players for the survival of the planet.

In return, students absorb problem-solving, reasoning and critical thinking skills.

By touching a boa constrictor; by viewing live insects under a microscope and by seeing a California Desert Tortoise or Moluccan Cockatoo right in the classroom, K-12 students naturally acquire meaningful educational experiences.

After their up-close-and-personal moments, students are actively engaged by the instructors to see the big planet picture of how some of these animals are endangered; how they must adapt to the loss of habitats and how the environment affects not only how we live but also how man needs to be ever diligent for the survival of every species, including our own.

Although this innovative program is only available to schools in Southern California, it is a model that could be replicated. For more information, contact Wildlife On Wheels, P.O. Box 152, Sunland, CA 91041 or call 818-951-3656.

"FAMILY MATH"
Teacher + Student + Parent
An Equation That Demystifies The Numbers

If math isn't adding up for your child or students, then consider starting FAMILY MATH in your school.

By having Mom or Dad in the classroom; by working with familiar objects and patterns and by eliminating possibilities, FAMILY MATH teaches K-8 students to *think* in a full circle about a singular math problem by using non-threatening, common sense logic that allows them to see "a supply of strategies ... relieving the frustration of not knowing how or where to begin," co-wrote founding director Nancy Kreinberg and acting director Virginia Thompson.

Within this interactive environment, FAMILY MATH is also highly flexible. It can be taught in any comfortable setting; by teachers; by teachers' aides; by a parent leading other parents and students; by community or company volunteers; by older adults or by older students.

This innovative learning experience is a classroom supplement that also pulls the parent into the school in a meaningful way on a regular schedule. It usually runs 4-8 weekly sessions lasting about 2 hours each. Classes can range from 5 to 200.

There are now over 40 sites around the U.S. where teachers or parents can take in-service workshops to get up and running. Training tools and materials are also available in Spanish.

If learning math in a family friendly environment computes, contact FAMILY MATH, Lawrence Hall of Science, University of California, Berkeley, CA 94720 or call 510-786-0941.

"Young Americans Bank"
Does More Math With $10 Savings Accounts

Here's another innovative way to teach math concepts.

Have students bank-by-mail at the Denver-based Young Americans Bank, the world's first and only FDIC-insured commercial bank for people under 22.

No waiting in line; savings accounts opened for a minimum of $10.00; checking accounts; loans; CDs; credit cards and ATM cards. All are accompanied with supplemental materials and careful instructions from staff.

Kids from all 50 states have opened accounts at an average age of 9 with an average balance of $454.

The bank's Education Foundation also offers a host of hands-on learning materials such as "Be Your Own Boss" and Financial Camps.

To open accounts for your students, contact Young Americans Bank, 311 Steele St., Denver, CO 80206 or call 303-321-2954.

"Correspondence With Correspondents"
Helps Students Learn Political Journalism

For open-minded high school students who are toying with career choices, the Public Broadcasting System's "Democracy Project" created a truly innovative way to go behind the scenes of political journalism.

Called "Correspondence with Correspondents," the project paired 15 leading political journalists with selected high school students in English, social studies and journalism classes from around the country.

After reviewing articles from the journalists, the students e-mailed or snail-mailed specific questions once a month about the stories they read. The reporters' direct answers gave students first-hand insight into the political process as well as a way to better understand the nuances of journalism.

Participants included political reporters from *The New York Times, Los Angeles Times, Washington Post, USA Today, Atlanta Journal-Constitution, San Diego Union-Tribune, Newsweek*, and *Time* among others.

Regardless of the size of the newspaper in your community, this electronic learning project — direct communications into the computers of hometown journalists — could easily be adapted to any school in the U.S.

"Playground Map"
Brings Geography Back
From The Siberia Of Education

When 50% of a *People* magazine poll said they thought Nicaragua was an alcoholic drink — and when high school students can't point to Canada on a map — it's time to re-focus on ways that will help bring geography back from the Siberia of education.

One novel approach creates a colorful, 20' x 30' "Playground Map" of the U.S. on local schoolyards so students can travel coast-to-coast and call out the states everyday at play.

Initiated by the Telephone Pioneers of America (the nearly 1 million retirees from the telecommunications industry), the map is drawn by first placing a master pattern of the nation on a newly-paved section of a playground. Then applying 6 gallons of primer and cans of (usually donated) white, red, green, blue, yellow and brown paint, the Pioneers make their "Picasso of the U.S."

While this isn't our father's way of learning geography, it's an innovative visual stimulator to get kids to start seeing the big picture.

To get this map permanently placed on your playground, contact Telephone Pioneers of America, 930 15th St., 12th Floor, Denver, CO 80202 or call 303-571-1200.

Photo by Valerie Krein

"Quilt Project"
Teaches 5 Lessons: Art, Creativity, Communication, Patience & Teamwork

With the patchwork lives many teenagers lead today, it only made sense that a patchwork quilt would help stitch together some elusive and difficult-to-teach themes of life.

Using the 1995 film "How To Make an American Quilt" as a backdrop, the joint effort brought together Debbie Joseph who was pursuing her master's degree in textiles at California State University at Northridge and teenagers from nearby Grant High School.

"Kids were able to see that all of their individual qualities can be used for the greater good," Joseph observed in the *Los Angeles Times*.

After dividing the quilt into 4 panels that illustrated the basic themes of air, earth, fire and water, Joseph then turned it over to the students who each had a 12-inch square to make their statement. Individual expressions included memories of a slain friend, a broken heart and motherly love which were symbolized by using buttons, photos and even corrugated cardboard with different types of fabric and stitches.

In the end, the huge quilt was a complete symbolic success for the mostly ethnic students. It permanently wove elements of art, creativity, communication, patience and teamwork into their gritty lives.

Art teachers in your school district could easily replicate this multidimensional learning experience.

"Floating Classroom"
Rolls On In Old Navy Vessel
What About HazMat Vehicles, Aircraft, Mfg. Plants?

On an 80-foot Navy training vessel that floats up and down the Ohio River, 100s of Pittsburgh students are learning real world applications of science and math as well as gaining critical thinking and teamwork skills.

In lieu of being sent to mothballs, the former training boat is now the halls of learning.

Known as the "Pittsburgh Voyager," the river program enables students to collect scientific information for a shipboard computer database that logs changes in the river's ecosystem. Students help each other by checking cloud conditions; calculating wind speeds and testing water for oxygen content.

What about retired fire trucks, police cars, haz mat vehicles, buses, airplanes, trolleys or even abandoned manufacturing plants that could be upgraded to provide exciting opportunities for students to learn the fundamentals on a variety of topics?

More novel ways of imparting the basics of education would give a fresh alternative to the traditional school rhythms that so often stifle interest.

Education must adapt to students' more sophisticated outside awareness to spike the learning process.

"Authentic 1-Room Schoolhouse"
Teaches History & Humility

Dipping their quill pens in ink pots; sitting on benches and facing blank, knotty pine walls, 3rd grade students in the 4 counties comprising the Rock Hill School District in South Carolina are literally going back to basics while learning some lifelong lessons along the way.

An 1840s, 1-room schoolhouse complete with an outhouse was a cooperative community construction project among Historic Brattonsville, the Rock Hill Applied Technology Center and school district carpenters. Students from the local schools rotate their visits to this living history lesson.

An authentic, pre-Civil War reproduction of an academy for well-to-do families, this school-away-from-school is run by teachers — wearing historically-correct dresses — who praise the students in the vernacular of the day. Lessons in penmanship, grammar, philosophy, history and other subjects are all taught in this time-tunnel atmosphere.

Students who are class wiseacres ruefully learn about dunce caps as the authenticity to detail drives home the message for those who snicker at the experience.

This sensible and affordable schoolhouse reproduction is a most innovative and creative way to teach the ever more pertinent subject of history.

For more information on how to re-create this model in your school district, contact Community Partnership Coordinator, Rock Hill School District Three of York County, 660 N. Anderson Rd., P.O. Drawer 10072, Rock Hill, SC 29731 or call 803-981-1000.

"The Concord Review"
Enables High School Students To Make Their Mark In History

As the only journal in the world that publishes the academic work of secondary students, *The Concord Review* has re-elevated the lost art of embracing history as a means to understand the nuances of current domestic and world affairs.

Founded by John Abele who helped steer Boston Scientific into prominence, *The Concord Review* has published over 352 historical essays with an average length of 5000 words from students in 36 states and 21 countries.

Teachers — who have access to the Internet — can download sample essays for use in their classes (or better yet, get a subscription) as well as hopefully motivate their students to enter submissions.

Awards of $2000 each are given "for student work of outstanding academic promise." Even if students don't win the monetary award, they can still use their published essay on college application forms.

For more information on helping students make their mark in history, contact *The Concord Review*, P.O. Box 661, Concord, MA 01742; call 800-331-5007 or visit their website at http://www.tcr.org.

CHAPTER 10

Raising Standards, Morale & Resources

Schools K-12

"The Center for Education Reform"
Helps Re-set The Compass Of Change

Now that the business world is feeling the full brunt of the long slide in public education, the debate on the management, standards and accountability of this $300 billion K-12 educational juggernaut is reaching a boiling point whistling out for massive but creative and effective change.

Pointing to the 21st Century, public education is facing a daunting confluence of debilitating factors: increasing enrollments, tighter budgets, tattered school buildings, stagnant test scores, a technology gap, bloated bureaucracies that clot change and defensive monopolies of power.

But public education is also facing the "C" word for the first time in its history. "C" as in competition.

These include: Charter Schools, Magnet Schools, Essential Schools, Private Contracting, Voucher Systems and School Choice amidst a concerted push toward more rigorous standards.

Blending these solutions to the myriad of problems is a bright light on the horizon.

For committed individuals, parents, teachers, community and business leaders who are catalysts for common sense change for a continuous rise in K-12 test scores culminating with high school graduates who have core competencies, consider contacting the prolific clearinghouse of low-cost, reform reprints, action papers, directories, info-packs and local success stories of results-oriented change that are available from The Center for Education Reform. (CER)

An independent, nonprofit educational lightning rod for re-setting the compass of the prevailing rigid mindset that governs our schools, CER only charges $1 to $10 for a range of publications that can begin to electrify the process of change in your school district.

For its "Publications Catalogue," contact The Center for Education Reform, 1001 Connecticut Ave., NW, Ste. 204, Washington, DC 20036; call 800-521-2118 or visit their website at http://edreform.com.

SCHOOLS #26

U S WEST Translates Federal Law Into English For K-12 Schools & Libraries Applying For $2.25 Billion In Funding

Talk about a life-saver for our beleaguered schools and libraries.

The Denver-based U S WEST Communications has come to the rescue not only for the schools in the 14 states it serves but also for public education throughout the nation.

As part of the 1996 Telecommunications Act, the federal government created a special provision known as Universal Service Funding for Education which provides $2.25 billion per year to 2001 for schools K-12 and libraries to purchase communication services and technology.

BUT the government's document on this Service Funding is 500 pages. Who at a school has the time to weave through it to properly complete the application? Not many, if any.

With an extensive commitment to electronically upgrade public education through its Connnected Schools program, U S WEST Communications has boiled down the essential elements of the process so

 schools everywhere can get busy with their applications.

Highlights of the streamlined presentation include:

- Discount Matrix on the "E-Rate"
- FCC Action Alerts
- Funding Application Worksheet
- Funding Application Technology Plan
- Funding Application RFP Template
- Requirements To Receive Funding

Updated as needed, this invaluable website will immensely assist motivated educators to take advantage of the $10+ billion available over the next 4 years. (The website also has links to 7 other funding sources.)

Go to http://www.uswesthomeroom.com/ and click on "The Bursar" to download all the details. Or contact Program Manager, Connected Schools, U S WEST Communications, 1801 California St., Rm. 1610, Denver, CO 80202 or call 800-DATA-USW.

"Great Kids Initiative"
Denver's Schools Compete
For Grants Up To $50,000 Each

A new source of funding that goes directly to individual school projects has been successfully introduced in Denver's secondary schools by Mayor Wellington E. Webb.

Webb's way is a creative redirection of Denver's Community Development Block Grants from the U.S. Department of Housing and Urban Development. With a pool of $500,000, this was the *first time* block grants were used for educational programs in Denver or any other major city.

Basic project criteria are:

- Must benefit at-risk students in schools K-12
- Must include community involvement
- Must target improved literacy scores or …
- Must target improved graduation rates

By keeping the criteria simple and the application streamlined to 3 pages, the "Great Kids Initiative" becomes a most innovative redirection of existing funding.

Sample projects have included:

• Asian Literacy Project	$50,000
• Environmental-Employment Preparation	25,000
• Literacy Through Technology Project	25,000
• Super Scholars Program	40,620
• Lunch Reading Buddies	2,250

For more information on this model program, contact the Great Kids Initiative, City and County of Denver, City and County Building, Denver, CO 80202 or call 303-640-3250.

300+ Websites Offer Links To Grants, Equipment, Resources & Projects For Teachers

The wacky World Wide Web is a wonderful window into resources, engaging classroom projects, equipment and technology for students and teachers, including tips on where to go for grant money!

Here are just a few:

ERIC at http://ericps.ed.uiuc.edu/ A mammoth clearinghouse on elementary and early childhood education, ERIC (Educational Resources Information Center) houses 750,000 documents such as the innovative "Regio Emilia Approach" from Northern Italy.

TEACHERS NETWORK at http://www.teachnet.org Has over 500 award-winning classroom projects; opportunities for the latest grants, contests, competitions and fellowships; a "Let's Talk" bulletin board discussing partnering with parents, leadership and technology and the "Blue Plate Special."

DONATION OF NASA PROPERTY & EQUIPMENT at http://www.hq.nasa.gov Besides an online curriculum for teachers, the NASA website has a link on how schools can acquire NASA property and technology. Over $75 million has been donated. Make your tax dollars work again, this time for public schools. (Also link to NASA's **http://www.teacherlink.usu.edu/** and **http://quest.arc.nasa.gov/**)

THE GLOBE PROGRAM at http://www.globe.gov Students and teachers from over 4000 schools in over 60 countries are working with research scientists to learn more about the planet Earth.

THE JASON PROJECT at http://www.jasonproject.org/ Each year, The JASON Project conducts a 2-week, live scientific expedition via satellite broadcast. Past expeditions include Iceland, Yellowstone and Journey From the Center of the Earth.

PBS TEACHER RESOURCE SERVICE at http://www.pbs.org
Electronic Field Trips, Instructional TV, Monthly Program Guide and PBS
Mathline are samples of the standards-based learning areas located at this
Public Broadcasting site.

**T.H.E. JOURNAL's ROAD MAP TO THE WEB FOR
EDUCATORS at http://www.thejournal.com** This huge guide lists over
300 education-related websites, including 23 on Grants and Funding alone.
Folded like a roadmap, the hard copy version is a must for teachers who
are searching the web for relevant sites for their students or themselves.
For more information, call 714-730-4011.

"FREE MATERIALS
For Schools & Libraries"
For Only $15 a Year

Professionally reviewed K-12 booklets, pamphlets and activity books such as the 103-page "Earth Day Teacher's Kit," the "Teacher's Packet of Geologic Materials" and "Billy Buck Hightrail's Mysterious Magical Garden" are all available for free to subscribers of this slim but mighty publication.

Unlike other lists, *FREE MATERIALS* promises that "short descriptions only are included since lengthy reviews for free materials are unwarranted in our opinion."

In one sample issue, 52 different materials were listed in 4 categories:

- Health & Nutrition
- Safety & Consumer Education
- Science
- Social Studies & Economics

For a publication that's published 5 times a year, it's the best $15 investment a parent, teacher or principal can make for their school.

For a subscription, contact *FREE MATERIALS For Schools and Libraries,* P.O. Box 34069, Dept. 349, Seattle, WA 98124 or call 604-876-3377.

Eliminate "Rich Kid/Poor Kid" Stereotypes By Sharing Resources At Public & Private Schools

Once upon a time, the public school students at Burbank Boulevard Elementary School thought their fellow private school students at the nearby Country School were different because "they're all rich kids."

Now — after 2 years of a unique sharing of resources between the schools — the students at the public school realize those rich kids "are just like us."

They also both learned that 1 + 1 = 3. That's the new math when a private school and a public school learn to erase stereotypes and help each other along the way.

Here's how the head of the private school made it work:

"When I was visiting my old alma mater, Burbank Boulevard Elementary, I was shocked at how badly their hands were tied in relation to resources," recalled Paul Singer. "There was no art program, no music program, no PE program, no computer program, overcrowded classrooms and textbooks that were 20-25 years old."

So he met with the principal at Burbank Boulevard and suggested that since his school didn't have an auditorium for assemblies, that they could set up a reciprocal agreement for sharing resources.

Now students from the public school are taking a 10-minute walk 2 to 5 times a week to the private school where they receive instruction in computers, art and PE in exchange for use of their auditorium by the kids at Country School. They've also conducted joint Christmas Caroling; co-hosted a golf tournament and paired up to help compose each other's biographies.

"This not only enriches each other's educational experience but it also helps break down stereotypes and misconceptions," added Singer who envisions a gradual expansion of this innovative exchange agreement.

For more information on sharing educational resources, contact Paul Singer, Country School, 5243 Laurel Canyon Blvd., Valley Village, CA 91607 or call 818-769-2473.

"ERASE"
Students' Pledge Drive To Eliminate Prejudice Delivers More Than a Promise

Teaching students that ...
We are *humans* who happen to be black or white;
We are *humans* who happen to be Asian or Hispanic;
We are *humans* who happen to be Jewish;
We are *humans* who happen to be blind;
We are *humans* who happen to be male or female ...
is a tough sell as there is so much bigotry baggage brought into the classroom.

Yet the students at a Northern New Jersey high school —disgraced by the national broadcast of some local white supremacist graffiti — banded together with the principal and a few teachers and created the rallying acronym of ERASE, End Racism And Sexism Everywhere, to clean the stain of a few town bigots.

Out of their fervor, more than 100 students drafted a unifying pledge:

"I, as a supporter of the ERASE program, pledge to use my best efforts to End Racism And Sexism Everywhere. I will get to know a person before I judge him or her. I will give everyone a chance to become all they are capable of being. When confronted with acts of prejudice or discrimination, I will not be silent. I will speak out."

Formed like an ad hoc Chess Club, the original ERASE program at Lakeland Regional High School has since been adopted by 23 other New Jersey schools.

Students in the ERASE program meet informally to vigorously chew through the issues of basic awareness, denial, gender bias, partner abuse and white power groups.

By adding monthly themes of Tolerance and Understanding into lesson plans; producing pamphlets; creating ERASE murals;holding Teen Summits; addressing Conflict Resolution and conducting Pledge Drives, this student program is effectively helping to erase perhaps the greatest obstacle preventing equitable progress in our society.

For more information about this breakthrough program that's applicable to any grade level, contact ERASE, 57 Boyle Ave., Totowa, NJ 07512 or call 201-595-5925.

========

Another excellent resource is Teaching Tolerance. Founded by the Southern Poverty Law Center in 1991, this project is dedicated to teaching inter-racial and inter-cultural understanding in the classroom and beyond.

For more information about their videos, posters and magazines, contact Southern Poverty Law Center, 400 Washington Ave., Montgomery, AL 36104 or call 334-264-0268.

"Circle Of Friends Club"
Closes Gap Between Disabled And Mainstream

Keeping developmentally disabled students separate from mainstream students in school is not productive for either group.

Linda Safan, a mother of a very shy boy with Down's Syndrome, recognized this. So she and Jacqueline Mink Close, the inclusion consultant at her son's school, started a group called the "Circle Of Friends Club"

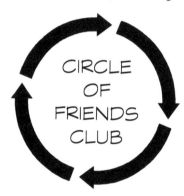

where students from both groups got to know each others' likes, dislikes, fears and emotions over lunch, special projects, photos, treats and trips.

The result?

Safan's son, Alec, became the first "full inclusion" student at Lincoln Middle School in Santa Monica, CA and the weekly club concept of "hanging out" has been implemented in 5 other schools.

What a simple yet sensible way of connecting the circle between these two usually isolated groups.

A few phone calls to volunteers and parents and a similar club could be breaking barriers and making new friends at a school in your community.

For more information, contact Jacqueline Mink Close, Department of Special Education, Santa Monica-Malibu Unified School District, 1651 16th St., Santa Monica, CA 90404 or call 818-829-8184.

"Total Quality Management"
Creates a Beacon In Brooklyn

Despite the pokey enthusiasm for the Total Quality Management (TQM) movement by American corporations, it has positively impacted schools. The trade magazine *Quality Progress* reported that over 415 schools, colleges and universities have used TQM.

One of the most sterling examples is the light emanating from the bleak battleship-gray doors at the 1700-student George Washington Vocational and Technical High School in Brooklyn, NY.

Initiated in January, 1991, TQM has been embraced with considerable zeal. The most compelling proof of the school's success was a student named "Ralph" from the Dominican Republic.

Ralph came to George Washington as a sophomore while his father was dying of Alzheimer's disease. "He basically gave up on school and became a drug dealer to support his father's hospital and doctors' bills," related Franklin P. Schargel, the school's former assistant principal. "After his father died, somebody identified him as a very bright student. He entered with a 41 average and graduated with an 84. Ralph then earned a Quality Improvement Scholarship to a prestigious technical school.

"Every month we target at least one problem area and direct our energies to removing its causes," added Schargel. "By identifying errors, locating and removing causes, we can change the atmosphere of the school for the better. The annual dropout rate went from 5.3% to 2.1% from 1991 to 1992; the PTA grew from 12 to 180 parents and a lunch time tutoring program helped cut the number of failing students from 151 to 11.

"It's working for our students; it's working for Ricoh (their school/business partner). And, although I do have that New York cynicism, it can work for America."

To bring TQM to your school, order *Transforming Education Through Total Quality Management: A Practitioner's Guide* by Franklin P. Schargel ($34.95) from Eye On Education, P.O. Box 388, Princeton Junction, NJ 08550 or call 609-799-9188.

It's Not Just a Car Wash;
It's The Principal!

When Cynthia Gladstone, principal of a continuation high school in Van Nuys, CA, was looking for a new way to motivate students who need serious motivation to graduate, she touched a nerve by offering to wash a student's car.

"I'm always looking for something to motivate these kids;taking them out to lunch; ice cream; something to reward them for making an effort," she explained.

"Every three weeks, they get a progress report with a number of points. When I told them I'd wash the car of the student with the highest number of points, I had no idea the interest would be so great."

"That day, they were doing things like squeezing the hose. I'd look at it and water would gush into my face. They loved seeing me make a fool of myself. It made me more human, more approachable.

"Also, they're so used to being anonymous. A lot of these kids have fallen between the cracks and don't have much faith in the system. But somehow this single event brought us all closer together. Unfortunately, they liked it so much they got the idea that the Principal's Car Wash was going to be every three-week period. I thought I had made it clear it was one-time only. Heck, I don't even wash my own car!"

What other motivational events can school principals and teachers do to make that human connection to students who just need that single spark to become more motivated?

Issue Shares Of Stock To "Shareholder" Parents & Students

Although overly maligned, public school teachers and administrators are by and large dedicated people who truly believe in the concept that educating students is an investment in the future.

From ages 5-18, our youth is in the hands of the public school system at least 40% of those years.

That's a considerable amount of time to allow any investment to appreciate.

At the beginning of elementary, middle and high school, why not issue "Shares of Stock" with the name of the school as the New York Stock Exchange "Corporation" and the names of the parent and student as the "Shareholders" of record?

It would help show parents that the school takes to heart its role of making individual students appreciate in value over the years. Seemingly, a local printer would be willing to donate the printing of authentic-looking shares of stock. Then the school could individually print in the names of the parents and students with a cover letter from the principal on the first day of school.

Let's make education the perennial "Bull Market" that it should be!

CHAPTER 11

Diffusing/Controlling Behavior

Schools K-12

Don't Let Scuffles Escalate
When You Can Mediate!
Philadelphia Program Has 92% Success Rate

Since 1984, a Philadelphia-based mediation program has been resolving spats in school before they become violent eruptions after school.

And it's most effective.

The program has a 92% success rate with youth-mediated agreements and a 85% success rate with adults who wish to settle their disputes.

"It's almost as if you're looking for the light bulb above their heads to start flashing," explained Cheryl Cutrona, executive director at the Good Shepherd Mediation Program, in the *Chestnut Hill Record*. "You see recognition in their eyes that maybe this is the first time that they really heard what the problems are."

Through her work as a mediator, Cutrona sees poor communication habits as the root of many problems. When dialogue deteriorates, no one hears the other side and that often escalates to violence.

Good Shepherd's primary program is a nationally-recognized "peer" mediation training class for grades 4-12. Student mediators get 24 hours of training with follow-up, feedback and, if necessary, re-training.

In "peer" mediation, a trained student (or teacher) typically has antagonistic students state their cases without being interrupted. Then the mediator tries to persuade them to come up with their own solution. Ideally, the mediator doesn't decide the dispute in either favor; he or she is there to facilitate conversation.

Over 43 Philadelphia public schools are using or implementing peer mediation programs in conjunction with Temple University and Good Shepherd.

In the Oakland (California) school district, the suspension rate fell 30% to 40% on most campuses that offered a similar mediation training for students and staff.

For information about this model program, contact Good Shepherd Mediation Program, 5356 Chew Ave., Philadelphia, PA 19138 or call 215-843-5413.

PeaceBuilders®
Puts Schoolyard Aggression Into Remission With Dramatic Changes In Elementary Behavior

In light of the sad statistic that our youth is now the most violent segment of society, a brighter and more hopeful light is beaming out of Tucson, AZ with the acceptance and proven results of the subtly powerful "PeaceBuilders" program.

Here are just two of its success stories:

- In Perris, CA, playground fights decreased from 125 to 23 and there was a 50% to 70% drop in classroom disruptions.

- At Emmerton Elementary in San Bernardino, CA, there was a 65% drop in student suspensions.

Essentially PeaceBuilders is a commitment to change hostile habits in grades K-5 with simple but sensible tools and rules of behavior and language that with diligent practice create a new peer standard that puts traditional schoolyard aggression into permanent remission.

Inspired by in-depth research and in alignment with recommendations from the American Psychological Association for the prevention of violent behavior in youth, 5 fundamental principles guide the PeaceBuilders program:

- Give Up "Put-Downs"
- Notice Hurts
- Praise People
- Right Wrongs
- Seek Wise People

These concepts are implemented through a comprehensive package of binders, handouts, kits, manuals, workbooks, videos and evaluation tools that can easily be blended into a Language Arts curriculum. (PeaceBuilders is not a curriculum but an environmental shift in behavior. It affects behaviors that predict violence and substance abuse and builds resiliency in children enabling them to have effective coping skills.)

Substituting the 1000s of acts of aggression a child absorbs through TV, movies, cartoons, toy commercials and schoolyard antics with daily acts of childhood civility is an effective, long-term way to make our kids "builders" of "peace" before they become adults.

This smart and savvy school program is a natural for nationwide implementation.

For more information, contact Heartsprings, Inc., the owner of the registered trademark of PeaceBuilders, at P.O. Box 12158, Tucson, AZ 85732; call 800-368-9356 or visit their website at http://www.peacebuilders.com.

(These trademarks can be used only by permission.)

"SECURITY DADS"
Roam At School Events; Rein In Unruly By Providing Multiplicity Of Father Images

You've probably seen those neon yellow jackets at sporting events with the words EVENT SECURITY on the backs of security personnel.

SECURITY DADS

Now take that concept into your local middle or high school where 33% to 50% of the students are from single parent (usually Mom) households. But instead of having anonymous paid security, have volunteer Dads wear your high school colors on T-shirts and jackets with the words SECURITY DADS emblazoned on the back.

Envision that and you'll have a powerful calming influence on your students.

This idea originated at the 1600-student body Arlington High School in Indianapolis, IN in 1991. Almost 30 Dads regularly don T-shirts and jackets; attend sporting events; chaperone at dances and make positive impacts on 100s of students who normally don't have a day-to-day Dad.

SECURITY DADS also fulfills an inclusion role for 30 fathers at Arlington High. "What guy wants to go to some PTA meeting and hear a bunch of women talk?" candidly asked first SECURITY DAD Anthony Wallace in *Parade Magazine*. "But give us something we can do, where we're really needed, and we'll be there."

For more information, contact SECURITY DADS, Arlington High School, 4825 N. Arlington Ave., Indianapolis, IN 46226 or call 317-226-3848.

School Dress Code Makes Fashionable Statement On Cutting Criminal Acts & Fighting By 36%

The common problems of public schools — crime, absenteeism, low test scores and peer pressures — have reversed their wicked ways through the mandatory wearing of uniforms in the elementary and middle schools of the Long Beach (California) Unified School District.

Once perceived as a cosmetic correction, the uniforms decreased overall incidents of fighting and other criminal acts by 36% in 9 categories from the 1993-94 to the 1994-95 school year, according to the *Los Angeles Times*. Plus, the policy has also lowered absenteeism and increased test scores as well as diffused those destructive jealousies among class levels.

Since everyone is dressed the same, the educational "playing field" is leveled. Without worrying about wearing certain brand name clothing, the students feel less intimidated and can focus more on their classroom performance. To help the poorest students maintain equality, service organizations and the PTA make sure every student is equally outfitted or at least has clean clothing.

Since Long Beach introduced its clothing standard, more than 400 out of the 660 Los Angeles Unified Schools have implemented uniform policies, according to the *Los Angeles Business Journal*. In addition, when undesirables wander onto school grounds, everyone can immediately spot those potential trouble-makers.

While uniforms are not the panacea to all of our public school problems, they do create an overall muted environment to temper tensions and allow schools to focus on other needed improvements to the learning process.

"Character Education"
5 Programs To Redefine Citizenship & Conduct

As most teachers say, "These kids weren't raised at my dinner table!"

Without pointing fingers, a few of the nation's schools have addressed the missing qualities of civility and ethics by implementing "Character Education" as a subject that's as crucial to student development as math and English.

And where it's been fully integrated, it's been a resounding success. To generate even more successes, here are 5 of the leading Character Education programs:

CHARACTER COUNTS!   Over 30 different colorful and creative teaching tools including audio and video tapes, bookmarks, lesson plans, pencils, posters, and T-shirts are available to help implement an all-encompassing, schoolwide character mentality that not only teaches students but also makes the educational staff accountable. All materials focus on the 6 pillars of character: Caring, Citizenship, Fairness, Respect, Responsibility and Trustworthiness. **For more information, contact CHARACTER COUNTS! Coalition, 4640 Admiralty Way, Ste. 1001, Marina del Rey, CA 90292 or call 310-306-1868.**

CHARACTER EDUCATION INSTITUTE   Offering customized character education lesson plans for K-6 and one for Grades 7-9, the San Antonio-based Character Education Institute (founded in 1942) has developed a "written-by-teachers-for-teachers" curriculum with activity sheets, discussion questions and character stories to read in class. One of the thought-provoking cartoon posters is titled "Are You Brave Enough To Be a Chicken?" **For more information, contact Character Education Institute, 8918 Tesoro Dr., Ste. 575, San Antonio, TX 78217 or call 210-829-1727.**

CHARACTER EDUCATION PARTNERSHIP   Offering a more academic approach, the Partnership provides a very detailed, 18-page "Character Education Resource Guide" that lists over 150 resources to help schools adopt Character Education. Many other in-depth services and programs are also available. **For more information, contact The Character Education Partnership, 918 16th St., NW, Ste. 501, Washington, DC 20006 or call 800-988-8081.**

DAYTON'S "WORD-OF-THE-WEEK"   There's a waiting list to enter some of Dayton's public schools; schoolwide tests scores are way up and students, for the most part, are on their best behavior. No it's not 1950 all over again; just the implementation and acceptance of a "character-related" word-of-the-week that only takes 10 minutes a day. Each week, one word — like Punctuality, Joyfulness, Patience, Self-Reliance, Neatness and Confidence —is introduced on Monday. The word is embraced all week with flyers; parental reading books to reinforce the word at home and 15-minute school plays dramatizing the word. During the 1996-97 school year, 37 words were thoroughly examined. **For more information, contact Allen Classical/Traditional Academy, 132 Alaska St., Dayton, OH 45404 or call 937-224-7364.**

STOP - THINK - ACT - REVIEW (STAR)   One of the original character education programs, STAR is a decision-teaching model that helps students solve problems and resolve conflicts with a calm, rational 4-step process. Developed by the Jefferson Center of Character Education, this nonprofit organization was founded in 1963. It now provides programs and publications such as the Principal's School Climate Handbook, Monthly Theme Bulletin Boards and 52 easy-to-follow "Lessons for Success" that blend into regular lesson plans. **For more information, contact the Jefferson Center of Character Education, 2700 East Foothill Blvd., Ste. 302, Pasadena, CA 91107 or call 626-792-8130.**

CHAPTER 12

Connecting Into Community

Schools K-12

"Service-Learning"
Maryland's Mandatory Requirement For Graduation Is National Model

Seeding the 6th through 12th graders in Maryland with the conviction that Civic Responsibility is a basic learned skill is a well-defined national model known as *"Service-Learning Education."*

Not a "filler" course and — since the 1993-94 school year, a mandatory requirement for graduation in 1997 and every year thereafter — Service-Learning is also NOT volunteering or community service. Here are the critical ground rules:

- Advance Learning
- Action
- Reflection

In each school district, these 3 criteria drive the locally designed programs which are accomplished by "making a difference through actions of caring for others through personal contact, indirect service or civic action, either in the school or in the community."

Examples of Service-Learning Education:

- Students studied aging and then interacted with older adults.

- Students worked with local government to stop illegal dumping.

- Students repaired donated cars and made them available to low-income families.

- Students lobbied a local legislature to pass a bicycle helmet law.

- Students produced and distributed a booklet on child abuse.

Although Maryland's implementation of mandatory Student-Learning Education was met with considerable initial hostility, it is definitely a bright example of a thoughtful way to plant Civic Responsibility as a lifelong commitment to our communities.

For more information, contact Luke Frazier, Executive Director, Maryland Student Service Alliance, Maryland State Department of Education, 200 West Baltimore St., Baltimore, MD 21201; call 410-767-0356; or visit their website at http://sailor.lib.md.us/mssa/.

"Class Action" Gives Students
Power To Get Connected

Students taking action to change laws or policy in the real world is a powerful learning tool for accelerating their assimilation into society.

For example:

- By circulating a petition, students at the Jackson Elementary School in Salt Lake City, UT had some nearby contaminated barrels removed. Then, after raising $2700 to donate to the state health department and subsequently finding there was no way to give the money for a specific purpose, 20 fifth and sixth-graders went to the state legislature; lobbied to change the law; got it passed and made the first donation.

- Six high school students spoke before the Los Angeles Board of Education and persuaded it to ban soccer balls from Pakistan and other countries believed to be using child workers.

- Since 1969, high school students in Fort Myers, FL have learned about participatory democracy and their local environment through the "Monday Group." After selecting a current environmental challenge, they tackle the project head on by meeting every other Monday. Results have included a manatee education site, recycling programs, ethanol production projects and saving the Six-Mile Cypress Swamp from development.

In elementary, middle or high school, students in every grade level are capable of focusing their energies on a single hometown topic and truly effecting change in the way adults run the world.

This is an untapped educational tool that can give students life-empowering skills. Rally the students around a cause and let them run with the ball!

========

Educators who want to seek creative ways students are taking action should consider the definitive and inspiring work of Wendy Schaetzel Lesko who compiled scores of examples of students making permanent differences in her book *No Kidding Around! America's Young Activists Are Changing Our World & You Can Too.*

Driven by a mission of "Democracy Dropout Prevention," Lesko is

also the founder of the ACTIVISM 2000 PROJECT designed to stimulate and encourage not only youthful activism but also serve as a wake-up call to the media and policy-makers to stop treating youth as a silent generation since 26% of the U.S. population is under 18 and underserved.

For more information and to order the book, contact ACTIVISM 2000 PROJECT, P.O. Box E, Kensington, MD 20895 or call 800-KID-POWER.

"MAGIC ME"
Unlocking Fears; Erasing Perceptions; Setting Free

Imagine a group of 10 to 15-year-olds from your middle school gagged and bound in chairs, motionless and speechless.

It kills them to sit there, immobilized, but they get the point.

This is the empathetic, bone-honest, 30-day training that at-risk students go through when they become a part of the highly-honored and powerful program called MAGIC ME that pairs them with older adults in a series of weekly, 1-on-1 human service exchanges from October through May.

When these opposite groups mix — youth with a self-centered dismissiveness of most of adult society and older adults who are routinely dismissed by most of society — not only are perceptions erased but also

Photo courtesy of MAGIC ME, Inc.

lasting and magical moments are created.

"Magic Me made me see there were great people trapped inside those decrepit old bodies," described one student in *Family Circle*. "Now I feel I can handle any kind of situation I meet in life. So many things I used to fear, I'm not afraid of anymore."

Created in 1980, MAGIC ME is a leading intergenerational exchange experience as graduates have less absenteeism, suspensions and better GPAs than control groups. Over 70 MAGIC ME programs are in place in the U.S. and Europe.

By enriching the lives of people who themselves often feel powerless, each group gives the other reciprocal reinforcement that elevates their own self-worth.

To start a MAGIC ME program in your school, contact MAGIC ME, Inc., 2521 N. Charles St., Baltimore, MD 21218 or call 410-243-9066.

========

In addition, there are over 350 intergenerational programs listed in *Young and Old Serving Together.* For ordering, contact Generations United, **c/o CWLA 440 11st St., NW, Ste. 310, Washington, DC 20001 or call 202-662-4283.**

"The Parent University"
Denver Suburb Emotionally Engages Parents Back To School

Responding to the statistic that 40% of high school parents never set foot in their child's high school, Debby Novotny — School/Community Partnership Coordinator at the Douglas County School District in the Denver suburb of Castle Rock — fulfilled a 2-year dream by establishing "The Parent University."

Designed to inform, involve and "connect with the community emotionally," The Parent University offers a variety of classes and workshops to teach parents how young people learn differently and how to engage them in a more active and meaningful way with the education of their son or daughter.

Within 3 weeks, the initial announcement about the university motivated over 500 parents to register for classes.

Sample courses include:

- Adolescent Emotions
- Conflict Resolution
- Emotional Intelligence
- Instructional Use of Internet
- Paired Reading
- Surviving the Teenage Years

Stretched over a 4-month period and taught primarily by school district personnel, The Parent University is "a non-threatening community builder and a powerful trust builder," according to Novotny.

For more information about this innovative way to engage parents back to school, contact Debby Novotny, Douglas County School District, 620 Wilcox St., Castle Rock, CO 80104 or call 303-814-5272.

Give Realtors a New Pitch: "Schools, Schools, Schools"

If schools hold "Open Houses" for parents, why not hold one for Realtors who are on the front lines of bringing new parents into your school district? One very community-minded school and Realtor Association did hold such an event and did so very successfully.

Cleveland High School in Reseda, CA held an Open House for 25 local Realtors and gave them an informal tour where students and teachers had a sparkling opportunity to display their innovative programs.

"Every Realtor should be knowledgeable about the schools located in the neighborhoods of the homes they're trying to sell so they can direct prospects on how to get more school information," explained Realtor Jay Tennen of Re-Max Center of Calabasas who organized the event as a member of the San Fernando Valley Association of Realtors. The first-of-its-kind tour was so successful that other local high schools were inspired to host similar events.

Want to start drawing quality children and parents to your school district? Give your local Realtors a new pitch: "Schools, Schools Schools."

Expand Schools Into
Community Centers & Partnerships

Imagine your school having weekend slumber parties so parents and kids can camp out and learn to communicate better.

Imagine your school having caseworkers on call 7 days a week.

Imagine your school offering community-wide immunization shots for toddlers.

Recognizing that schools can no longer operate in isolation from the families of its students and the community, a model program in St. Louis is changing the perception of schools by working in the true spirit of "taking a village to rear a child."

Started in 1989, the "Caring Communities Programs" have expanded into 18 St. Louis schools which are open from 6:30 a.m. to 9:30 p.m., Monday through Friday.

Prevention and intervention programs include:

• Afterschool tutoring
• Case management
• Cultural classroom presentations
• Drug and alcohol counseling
• Health fairs, outreach and screening
• Latchkey
• Pre-employment/job placement
• Recreation
• Respite nights
• Teen leadership

For more information on one of the pioneers of bundling community services into schools, contact the Caring Communities Programs, 4411 N. Newstead St. Louis, MO 63115 or call 314-877-2050.

========

Other Community-School organizations to contact:

COMMUNITIES IN SCHOOLS   This nationwide stay-in-school program centers its concept on a "Community Coach" whereby an individual at the school is designated to connect the community and its resources to young people. **For more information, contact Communities In Schools, 1199 N. Fairfax St., Ste. 300, Alexandria, VA 22314 or call 703-519-8999.**

NATIONAL ASSOCIATION OF PARTNERS IN EDUCATION, INC. (NAPE)   Connecting children and teachers with corporate, education, volunteer, government and civic leaders whose collective mission is to improve the content and delivery of education services is the 7500-member NAPE. Its in-depth symposiums and information exchanges form an exceptional sharing network of innovative ideas that are easily replicated. **For more information, contact NAPE, 901 N. Pitt St., Ste. 320, Alexandria, VA 22314 or call 703-836-4880.**

NATIONAL CENTER FOR COMMUNITY EDUCATION (NCCE)   This organization has a guide that gives 1-page profiles of "135 Community/School Partnerships That Are Making a Difference." **For a free copy, contact NCCE, 1017 Avon St., Flint, MI 48503 or call 810-238-0463.**

NATIONAL COMMUNITY EDUCATION ASSOCIATION (NCEA)   Formed to solidify parent and community involvement in public education, the NCEA has numerous programs, resources, guides, videos, manuals and journals that help make schools more of a centerpiece in the community. **For an information packet, contact NCEA, 3929 Old Lee Highway, Ste. 91-A, Fairfax, VA 22030 or call 703-359-8973.**

PACIFIC CENTER FOR VIOLENCE PREVENTION   Recognizing that youth are more likely to commit crime at 3 p.m., full-service schools identified as "Beacon Centers" in New York City, "YouthNet Centers" in Chicago, "Village Centers" in Oakland and "Second Shift Schools" are springing up in major urban communities. **For more information, contact Pacific Center for Violence Prevention, San Francisco General Hospital, San Francisco, CA 94110 or call 415-285-1793.**

"Principal for a Day"
Schools Should Immediately Ink It In

A casually underwhelming way to get busy corporate executives and community leaders personally involved in public education is to hold an annual "Principal for a Day" event where the guests are under no obligation to commit money or resources but — because of making that personal connection — are so energized they often over-extend themselves.

Take Beverly Chell, vice chairman of K-III Communications. After hearing first-hand from students about their woeful lack of books during her stint as Principal for a Day, she marshaled the resources to collect and distribute over 1 million books to New York City's public schools.

This and many other spillover contributions occurred spontaneously because of a nonprofit called Pencil — Public Education Needs Civic Involvement In Learning.

Formed in 1995, Pencil is an exquisitely simple but brilliant idea to engage prominent New Yorkers — such as Richard Avedon, Edgar Bronfman Jr., Bill Cosby, Walt Frazier and Jane Pauley — as well as 1000 other individuals from the private and public sectors to teach class; share lunch; sit on Student Council; read; attend an assembly; conduct a conflict resolution discussion and just basically get involved by engaging in the daily lives and times of today's students who are potentially that guest Principal's future employees.

Not just a PR photo op, Principal for a Day has multiple K-12 cross-cultural ripple connections that have developed long after the day ended. These include career counseling, donations, internships, mentoring, scholarship funds/grants and workplace visits to name a few.

Imagine the community synergy that could be created if your school district had just 50 Principals for a Day. For many students and schools, this innocent event could turn into a new direction for life.

For more information, contact Pencil, Inc., Park Ave. Plaza, 55 East 52nd St., 29th Floor, New York, NY 10055 or call 212-909-1720.

High School Spanish Students Serve As Translators; Tighten Communications At Local Hospital

Doctors' communications to patients have never been a hallmark of efficiency in health care.

Exacerbate that poor track record in a community where 60% of the population is Spanish-speaking and you've got *muchos mas* chances for miscommunications.

Although the Santa Paula Hospital in Santa Paula, CA has numerous employees who speak Spanish, it's often not enough to fill the gaps during off hours and on weekends.

"We now have 30 Advance Placement Spanish students who earn 6 units by volunteering as translators," explained Laya Murphy, education coordinator, who founded the program. "They have to sign a code of conduct; must always be professional and are on call for four hours of duty."

The students are equipped with pagers to come in and volunteer their bilingual skills in the emergency room, radiology department and laboratory. The students get a skill experience for their resumes and hospital employees have more time for their specific tasks.

Seemingly, this simple solution to a growing problem could be incorporated by any Spanish Language Department in any U.S. high school as most major urban areas are experiencing increasing Hispanic populations.

It could even be adapted to police departments, paramedics and 911 operators who need bilingual translators to speed their communications in emergencies. There are multiple winners in a community when students act as translators at public health and emergency agencies.

For more information, contact Laya Murphy, Education Coordinator, Santa Paula Hospital, P.O. Box 270, Santa Paula, CA 93061 or call 805-525-7171.

SCHOOLS #49

"Elder Education Corps"
Drive Miss Daisy Back To School

Two segments of society that could benefit more from each other are the burgeoning older adult population and public school children.

Call it the "Untapped Generation" helping the "Strapped Generation."

Imagine your community with a well-organized corps of older adults who could go to schools in bus brigades and offer their prisms of patience and tolerance to students.

Imagine students gaining new respect for these elderly role models from regular exchanges of the small miracles in life as well as from their insightful mentoring.

Imagine a happier, more fulfilled older adult population which could feel more useful to society. Is it too simple a concept?

In some areas, it's already working. For example, the Los Angeles Public Library System has the "Grandparents and Books" program which has 500 grandparents reading to children after school. Initiated in 1989, the program is now in more than 100 locations throughout the state. Nearly everywhere these intergenerational programs have been tried, they've been quite successful.

It could begin by just a phone call from the school district to a senior organization or vice versa.

Start it, sustain it and it will flourish!

PART IV

Individual

Here are 49 programs, projects, ideas or suggested changes in your daily rhythms that can singularly or collectively upgrade the satisfaction, meaning and quality of your life.

In Chapter 13 titled "From Me To We," there are 20 thought-provoking ways to make this concept a permanent lifestyle change. Many of these are easy-to-put-your-arms-around, backyard, neighbor-to-neighbor, family, friend or small informal group ideas whose common denominator is to motivate an individual away from an inward concentration into a consistently outward, caring connection.

This concept of From Me To We was created by Nancy Geyer Christopher, author of *Rights of Passage: The Heroic Journey to Adulthood.* Christopher itemizes 7 steps on the "journey from me to we" where children learn to shed their self-absorption and wear a new coat of concern for others.

This same principle needs to be ingrained in individuals of all ages whereby we sometimes just need a creative push to nudge us out of our predominantly selfish ways.

In Chapter 14 titled "Digging In For Earth & Wildlife," there are 9 global outreach organizations or at-home projects that need committed individuals to help preserve the trilogy of balance among man, wildlife and the environment.

In Chapter 15 titled "20-Point Front-End Alignment," there are 20 suggestions on how to make small adjustments for a better quality life and how to craft a higher level of interpersonal relations.

The rest is up to you. Whichever ones you choose to pursue, do them now because a little bit of the future slips away everyday!

CHAPTER 13

From Me To We

Individual

LEADERS ARE READERS ...
"The Incredible Reading Rally!"
Help Destroy the Enemy Within

Imagine combining the state populations of ...

Arizona	Idaho	Maine	Nebraska
Arkansas	Iowa	Massachusetts	Nevada
Colorado	Kansas	Missouri	New Mexico
Connecticut	Kentucky	Montana	North Dakota
Hawaii			

which total 44 million, and you've got some idea of how many people in the U.S. have significant literacy needs.

Illiteracy is a lifetime sentence to multiple vulnerabilities inflicted on one's self and to others. For example, illiteracy causes bad decision-making as others prey on people who can't read contracts; the voting of shady propositions or candidates with uninformed judgments; an ignorance of product recalls; an inability to comprehend changes in traffic or weather conditions and a lack of awareness of health care alerts or new medical treatments.

To help destroy this silent enemy within, the Literacy Volunteers of America, Inc. (LVA) has created a national 2-week reading blitz called "The Incredible Reading Rally!" Volunteers seek pledges and read as many books as they can to a child, friend, patient or student.

To get involved in this annual event, contact LVA, 635 James St., Syracuse, NY 13203 or call 888-472-5599.

Other worthy groups to contact:

The Barbara Bush Foundation   **202-955-6183**
for Family Literacy
1112 16th St., NW, Ste. 340
Washington, DC 20036

Laubach Literacy Action   **315-422-9121**
1320 Jamesville Ave.
P.O. Box 131
Syracuse, NY 13210

National Institute for Literacy   **800-228-8813**
800 Connecticut Ave., NW, Ste. 200
Washington, DC 20006

National Center For Family Literacy   **502-584-1133**
325 West Main St., Ste. 200
Louisville, KY 40202

Rolling Readers   **800-390-READ**
P.O. Box 4827
San Diego, CA 92164

Root Out Hunger At Ground Level ...
Gardeners Can Contribute
With 1 Extra Row

There are approximately 100 million gardeners in the U.S.

There are approximately 30 million hungry people in the U.S. In addition, a late 1997 survey by the U.S. Conference of Mayors reported that 86% of our cities were experiencing an increase in demand for emergency food assistance.

Now in a deceptively simple but exponentially powerful campaign, gardeners can systematically address the pangs of hunger with an extra row.

Created by the Garden Writers Association of America (GWAA) in 1995, this common sense campaign — whose seeds of instruction can be picked up by anyone with a backyard — has caught on with a flourish and an accelerated growing pattern.

Joan Jackson, garden editor for the *San Jose Mercury News*, motivated her readers to pledge 34,000 pounds in 1995 and almost doubled that production with pledges of 64,000 pounds in 1996.

By intercropping and planting closer together, gardeners can take their carryover crops to a Second Harvest outlet or Foodchain distribution center. **For hometown locations, call Second Harvest at 312-263-2303 or 800-532-FOOD or call Foodchain at 800-845-3008.**

For more information about the "Plant a Row For the Hungry" campaign, contact the Garden Writers Association of America, 10210 Leatherleaf Ct., Manassas, VA 20111 or call 703-257-1032.

Let Your Voice Speak Volumes For The Blind & Dyslexic

Anyone ever comment on the melodic tone of your voice?

If so — and you don't sound like Cruella in "101 Dalmatians" — and you'd like to make a statement for the 4.8 million blind and millions more who have some form of reading disability, then consider becoming a volunteer for Recording For The Blind & Dyslexic.

 **RECORDING FOR THE BLIND & DYSLEXIC**

Since this sight-impaired group is pursuing college, post-graduate and lifelong learning in droves, they need volumes and volumes of textbooks.

Current volunteer needs are for people who can regularly record for a minimum of 2 hours a week and who ideally have professional experience in the following areas:

- Accounting
- Business
- Computers
- Economics
- Health Care
- Math
- Medicine

After completing an audition, committed orators must not only read text like fluid pearls of wisdom but also paint word pictures of accompanying graphs, charts and illustrations. Although it's definitely not recreational reading, there are more than 30 subject areas to connect to your best vocal instincts.

So if you'd like to give it a go where the internal rewards are high and the need is great at all of the organization's 30 recording studios across the U.S., then give them a call and let your voice cascade over a textbook on foreign policy, economics, basic English, physics or the latest in organic chemistry among others.

For an introductory pamphlet and the location of the studio nearest you, contact Recording For The Blind & Dyslexic, 20 Roszel Rd., Princeton, NJ 08540; call 609-452-0606 or visit their website at http://www.rfbd.org.

"Compeer"
Be a Mental Mentor;
It's Much More Personal Than Prozac

Mental illness is not the hush-hush disease anymore.

With 40 million Americans suffering from over 400 types of mental illness — such as panic disorder, mood disorder, schizophrenia and depression among others — treatments combining therapy and popular medications such as Prozac are enabling many patients to confront their disease; overcome it and get back into the mainstream.

 Enhancing traditional psychological and medically-prescribed treatments is an award-winning, highly-effective, low-cost program — known as Compeer — that uses trained and screened volunteers as steady, nurturing mentors who provide the missing link of personal friendship that is so essential to shepherd individuals into less chemical dependency. Or as Cicero once observed, "Friendship doubles our joy and divides our grief."

With 119 Compeer affiliate programs around the U.S., volunteers can connect in many major metropolitan areas and begin the interview and training process. After a match is made, Compeer volunteers are expected to visit their client a minimum of 4 hours a month for a year by doing a variety of social activities.

Now in its 25th year, the nonprofit Compeer has a greater need for volunteers than ever before, especially with the high cost of institutional treatment. Depending on the location, Compeer mentoring friendships only cost $375 to $1100. (Volunteers of course do not pay this fee.)

However it's money well invested. Based on a 1996 survey, Compeer friendships fostered a *51% reduction* on the client's rate of re-hospitalization.

If you would like to get involved with this highly-satisfying program, contact Compeer Program, Inc., Monroe Square, B-1, 259 Monroe Ave., Rochester, NY 14607; call 800-836-0475 or visit their website at http://www.compeer.org.

Reinvigorate Your Alumni Chapter With Meaningful Community Service

As a way of bonding beyond Homecoming, alumni associations have tapped into community service projects as a way to strengthen ties back to the alma mater.

Examples of Alumni Community Service Projects:

- Career Day at local high school
- Collecting coats for homeless at Homecoming game
- Golf Tournament for Alzheimer's research
- Outings for older adults
- Plugging into national projects such as Special Olympics
- Refurbishing a Homeless Shelter
- Students "Shadowing" alumni at offices
- Volunteering at Public TV Pledge Drive

"In communities across the nation, clubs — and the alumni administrators back on campus who help organize them — have found that community work provides the added purpose that some groups have traditionally lacked," wrote Jennifer Jackson Sanner in *CASE Currents.*

"Football and basketball parties alone won't build a strong club. But a community service goal can galvanize a diverse group, sustain loyalty and extend the reach and reputation of even the most prominent institution. Good deeds feed not only the soul but also the mind."

Some of the active community service alumni associations include Boston College, Bowling Green, Claremont McKenna, Duke, North Carolina, Notre Dame, Texas, Washington, UCLA and Smith College among many others.

So if your alumni association hasn't given it the old college try with this form of "Continuing Education," then pick up the ball with your chapter.

Raise a Dog For 15 Months And Enhance a Person's Independence For 8 Years!

Calling all dog lovers, especially if you adore Golden Retrievers, Labrador Retrievers, Shelties or Pembroke Welsh Corgis.

CANINE COMPANIONS
FOR INDEPENDENCE

If one of these is your favorite breed and you want to do a good deed, then consider becoming a "Puppy Raiser" for Canine Companions for Independence.

These dogs are not only eternally cheerful but they can also become personal valets by turning on lights and doing other minor chores or they can become savvy fire protectors by warning a hearing impaired person of a buzzing smoke alarm. But before these dogs become safety latches, they must be reared properly in a volunteer Puppy Raiser's home.

There are 4 types of dogs needed for this nationwide program that has "companions" waiting for their "canines." They are:

- **Assisted Service Dogs**   Act as true companions for children with disabilities or people with developmental disabilities.

- **Facility Dogs**   Enhance quality of life for people by working with professional caregivers.

- **Hearing Dogs**   Act as alert ears for deaf people or someone who is hard of hearing.

- **Service Dogs**   Perform tasks for people in wheelchairs or who have serious mobility limitations.

When the carefully selected 8-week-old puppy arrives at your home, you are expected to shower considerable love and attention over the next 14-17 months.

You'll also teach the dog basic obedience skills to build its confidence to be a responsive and caring canine. Puppies can accompany you to work and sleep quietly under your desk while patiently waiting for your command.

They're also expected to sleep in your bedroom as well as attend public events to learn to stay alert in crowds.

Then after it's reared with those good social graces, you return the dog for 6 months of advanced training before it moves on to Team Training with its future partner. Upon graduation, you, as the Puppy Raiser, proudly hand over the leash to a most appreciative Companion.

If you want to share these moments of joy, contact Canine Companions for Independence, P.O. Box 446, Santa Rosa, CA 95402; call 800-572-2275 or visit their website at http:// www.caninecompanions.org/

"Nonprofit Registry"
Have Guests Re-gift Wedding Or Anniversary Presents Into Nonprofit Donations

Inspired by his sense of activism against injustice, TV producer and part-time teacher Gary Krane raised eyebrows and the collective consciousness of more than just 80 family members and friends when he and his fiancee, Karen Ehrlich, mailed out their wedding invitations.

On the front of the card was a modified quote from Tolstoy that read: "The purpose of a GREAT MARRIAGE is not only to give each other joy & support, but also, together, to bring more courage, truth & justice into the world."

With that cue, they directed guests to select a nonprofit group from a list of 18; write a check and bring it to their wedding reception which was held on April 20, 1997.

Their "Registry" categories included:

- Protection of Children   (4 choices)
- Protection of Democracy   (5 choices)
- Protection of Environment   (5 choices)
- Protection of Homeless   (4 choices)

After the initial shock waves reverberated throughout their respective family members, everyone came through with checks ranging from $10 to $200 for a total of $2000.

"Even in our greatest joys in life, we must never forget the suffering of those less fortunate around us," Krane told his guests at the wedding. "That has been for 1000s of years a very Jewish attitude, and one, in my opinion, we should be very proud of, but one, very sadly, many of us have forgotten in the prosperity and narcissism of the 80s and 90s. And I believe responsibility to help the less fortunate is basic to most religions."

One of the surprises from their creative wedding was the number of discounts and outright donations they received from vendors who were so taken with their community-directed gesture. These included a gorgeous location overlooking the Pacific Ocean that would have normally cost $1000 and the donated services of 2 professional photographers.

Considering the millions of excessive and expensive gifts that are dutifully brought to weddings and anniversaries throughout the U.S., a widespread adoption of this sensible redirection would naturally do wonders for the nonprofit community. But perhaps more importantly, it might make a habit-changing statement to guests to think and act more responsibly while rekindling a spark for humanity that is within all of us.

For information on how to have "A Wedding Or Anniversary For Just Causes," contact Gary Krane, Ph.D., 4419 Tyrone Ave., Sherman Oaks, CA 91423 or call 818-783-7489.

Stand Up For The 500,000 Children Bouncing Around Foster Care Pinball

Bouncing around courts and foster homes can make children feel like battered pinballs.

Unfortunately, over 500,000 children are reeling back-and-forth from slot to slot and eventually they become criminals. (According to *Marie Claire*, 80% of America's prison inmates are former foster children.)

Their only way out is through the overworked and underappreciated social worker who typically handles 45 to 90 cases. So at a time of life when children need constant attention, foster children receive negligible individual concern and instead are in constant rotation.

But now committed community volunteers can become a continual presence and conscientious voice for these kids. People who want to stand up for a single child can become a trained Court Appointed Special Advocate or CASA.

Essentially, CASA volunteers are appointed by a judge to be an advocate for 1 child — or 1 sibling group — acting as the eyes and ears of the court. After researching information and talking to everyone involved with a child, volunteers make recommendations to help establish some semblance of childhood.

No special experience is required but advocates make a commitment to the child for the life of a case. That time will vary but most programs ask for 24 months of singular devotion. There are approximately 38,400 CASA volunteers in 678 programs across the U.S.

To become a CASA volunteer, ask for a list of the CASA offices in your state by contacting The National Court Appointed Special Advocate Association, 100 West Harrison St., North Tower, Ste. 500, Seattle, WA 98119; calling 800-628-3233 or visiting their website at http://www.nationalcasa.org.

========

An organization that guides older foster children into independent adulthood is The Orphan Foundation of America (OFA). **For more information, contact OFA, 380 Maple Ave., West, Ste. LL5, Dept. P, Vienna, VA 22189; call 800-950-4673 or visit their web-site at http://www.orphan.org.**

"Offspring Day"
A New Tradition
To Keep Your Family Tightly-Knit

It started in 1955.

On a Sunday in July, Raquel Beaumont put a rose by the napkin of each daughter and a carnation by the napkin of each son.

All 5 children looked at each other wondering what the heck was going on at their small home in Arleta, CA.

Raquel explained she was starting a new tradition and it would be called "Offspring Day." Every year at this time, she would honor her children with a special day. The only gifts provided would be time and love and, of course, the appropriate flower by their napkins.

"When we see children in gangs today or doing something wrong, we know it is the parents who failed," observed one of Raquel's daughters, Carmen Cordova, in an article in the *Daily News* by Dennis McCarthy, a 3-time winner of the "Best Columnist" award from the California Newspaper Publishers Association.

"You must be strict with your children, but they must feel your love, too. You must give them patience and attention. Don't waste the minutes you sit and talk with your children. Make them important. Make them count."

There are now 35 grandchildren and great-grandchildren in the Beaumont family circle. All are part of this annual event that's been held for over 40 years.

What an innovative and meaningful homegrown tradition that any family could easily start. All it takes are time, love, a rose and a carnation.

Teach Bored Children To *Think* (What a Concept) And Have Fun ... With Board Games

Okay, so you're a pretty good chess, bridge or canasta player. But you're also a concerned citizen worried about children in your hometown who are growing up without critical thinking skills.

Then do what Carl Hanna did in Gastonia, NC.

He contacted his local elementary schools and offered to teach students how to play chess. More than a 100 kids checkmated him with a positive response.

Hanna subsequently opened his home as a chess classroom; provided all the chess equipment and even brought in chess instructors from Charlotte. Hanna's hunch is paying off as he sees growth in the analytical skills of his students. "One student born with a learning disability," he proudly told *Modern Maturity*, "has been rated an expert at chess."

Three separate studies corroborate Hanna's volunteer work by showing that students who learn chess have better reading scores, cognitive development and critical thinking skills.

Sure it's not going to pull the masses off the next Disney marketing blitz, but if enough conscientious board game players took this same effort to steer children to the creative challenges of these games, then we might uncover a few geniuses along the way. It's your move.

Teach The Lessons Of "Spending, Investing & Charity" With 3 Little Banks

Charity not only begins at home but it can be taught for a lifetime with the simple and innovative designation of a special piggybank for planting the seed of philanthropy in your children.

"Everytime one of my three-year-old twins earns a quarter or a dollar, they have three piggybanks to choose from," outlined Joy Prefer Cohen, a regional sales director for Smith Barney, Inc. in Studio City, CA.

"I told them they have one piggybank for saving money to spend on a gift or toy; they have another piggybank for investing to let money grow for college and they have a third piggybank to collect money for people who need help.

"I wanted to instill in my children early on the value of money and how to be a responsible person by developing financial security. Part of that is allocating a portion of their money for charitable organizations and events."

Even though some of Cohen's friends and acquaintances have chuckled at her piggybanks, since she started in 1996 she's seen the light of understanding emanating from Gabrielle and Gregory as they chatter to each other on where to put their latest collection of dollars and cents. And for Cohen, that's all that counts.

Photo by Delmar Watson

Make Play Paramount In a Child's Life

Restoring the mundane miracle of purposeless play in a child is absolutely critical as a precursor to a more productive and fulfilling life not only for children but also for adults.

"One of the most essential characteristics to a meaningful life is that of joy — joy brought about by a spirit of playfulness," stated Maria T. Allison, Ph.D. at Arizona State University in her book *Play, Leisure and Quality of Life.*

Unfortunately actual play time is downsizing because of the continuing electronic intrusion of TV, videos, CD games and the unproductive use of the PC as passive or non-social diversions. Since play is the naturally dominant behavior mode of a child for at least the first 5 years of life, encourage it and enhance it wherever possible.

"We have 30-year-olds having heart attacks and teenagers committing suicide," noted Professor Jan Tolan at California State University on the Northridge campus. "We have all these people saying, 'This isn't fun anymore.' Juvenile delinquents don't have role models who enjoy life. Children need role models who enjoy their life or they don't see any reason to grow up. That's why the play ethic has to be instilled early for it to carry through life and to have balance in our lives."

Literally *100s* of research studies have proven how consistent, uninhibited play among children acts as an incubator for numerous lifelong benefits.

20 Proven Benefits To Childhood Play

Better control of impulses	Less aggression/stress
Better emotional adjustment	More creativity
Better problem-solving	More curiosity
Better peer cooperation	More empathy
Better verbalization	More flexibility
Greater concentration	More friendships
Greater vocabulary	More group activity
Higher intellectual competence	More self-esteem
Higher language comprehension	More sense of community
Higher language level	More sharing

"Trips For Kids"
Use Pedal Power To Pump Self-Confidence Into Inner-City Youth

If you're a biking enthusiast *and* ...

You want to create a positive program for youth in your hometown, then contact "Trips For Kids" and learn how you could easily adapt it to your area.

It is the epitome of blending your favorite recreation into an humanitarian exercise.

With donated mountain bikes and helmets, Trips For Kids kickstarts on weekends by collecting 12 disadvantaged children ages 10-17 and then taking them to a local mountainous trail where they challenge themselves to get to the top of the hill.

Before riding starts, biking etiquette lessons from the International Mountain Biking Associates Rules of the Trail are delivered along with basic environmental education.

"When they learn they can make it to the top of the hill, they also learn they can do that in life," reflected Marilyn Price in *Who Cares* magazine. Since she founded the nonprofit Trips For Kids in 1988, Price and her program leaders have taken more than 3000 inner-city kids to the top of that proverbial hill.

For more information, contact "Trips For Kids," 138 Sunnyside, Mill Valley, CA 94941; call 415-381-2941 or visit their website at http://www.webcom.com/tfk.

Access A La Carte, Just-Show-Up Volunteering Via "doingsomething," L.A. Works & Websites

Too busy to fit volunteering into your busy schedule?

Now there's a way to start reaping the personal benefits of volunteering without some big organizational extravaganza on your part.

It's a nonprofit group called "doingsomething" that mails a monthly newsletter of flexible, 2-4 hour volunteer activities for busy professionals.

The newsletter details 15-20 upcoming community volunteer events by listing the name of the group, location of the event, background, time, task, number of volunteers needed and the project leader to call. Then you commit 2 hours; collect the internal rewards of volunteering and, perhaps, 2 weeks later sample another group.

Although there are "doingsomething" groups in only 2 cities — Washington, DC at 202-393-5051 and Los Angeles at 310-391-3907 — consider organizing a group in your community by checking out the Washington website at http://www.doingsomething.org.

========

Another similar organization is the flexible L.A. Works which creates "hands on" community service projects arranged to fit working schedules. Participation in its annual L.A. Works Day has increased every year from 1500 to 4100 volunteers. **For more information, call 213-936-1340.**

========

Also, web savvy volunteers can go to 5 sites that list hometown volunteer activities. They are:

http://www.americaspromise.org
http://www.idealist.org
http://www.impactonline.org
http://www.netday.org
http://www.servenet.org

INDIVIDUAL #15

Retire ... But Stay In The Loop

"I've worked at about 15 nonprofit agencies since I retired from Rockwell in 1986," proudly stated 80-plus Bob Holbrook of Brentwood, CA.

"Teaching the basic principles of good management and the fundamentals of human resource policies combined with the receptiveness and eagerness to learn at organizations like the Mexican American Legal Defense And Educational Fund makes you feel good."

Anne Bunney, a former clinical psychologist, gave up her private practice after the death of her husband. But she started volunteering her professional skills at the St. Joseph Center in Santa Monica and it was the antidote she needed.

"I felt it would be part of my healing process and I wanted to give back to the community," Bunney said. "It doesn't feel like work. It's so exciting. It's so rewarding. I believe everybody can make a difference."

Holbrook, Bunney and 1000s of other retired professionals are "911" volunteers "on call" at the nonprofit Executive Service Corps to go into the community and help nonprofit organizations redefine their missions; stimulate fundraising; develop strategic marketing plans and provide a sense of hope and renewal.

In the years to come, they'll need it to head off the coming crisis in nonprofit agencies. Based on a national study of 100 charitable organizations by Independent Sector, nonprofits will face a $254 billion cumulative gap in funding during the fiscal years 1996-2002.

There are Executive Service Corps (ESC) affiliates in 46 cities around the country.

For more information about joining ESC in your community, contact the National Executive Service Corps, 257 Park Ave. South, New York, NY 10010 or call 212-529-6660.

Other organizations offering retirees the "psychic income" of volunteering include the Service Corps of Retired Executives (SCORE) at 800-368-5855 and the Foster Grandparent Program at 800-424-8867.

"Neighborhood Book Review Club"
Start One With Your Literate
(Or Even Semi-Literate) Friends

If TV and movies have patronized you one too many times, then consider a "Neighborhood Book Review Club" that fulfills a couple of neglected needs.

It first gives you a new raison d'être to tighten the bonds on a loose group of 4 to 8 friends when you've run out of ideas on how to get together more often.

Secondly, it expands your horizons as you gain valuable insights and knowledge into history or contemporary culture. Your guilt at your lack of lifelong learning will now be somewhat mitigated and you'll have something garden-fresh to discuss at lunches, dinners and soirees.

Here's how Jim Haun of Pacific Palisades, CA described his club in the *Los Angeles Times*:

> "About the intellectual level of our reading group someone else will have to judge, but we're surely contenders in the number of meetings department. We began in September, 1965, and we meet weekly on Tuesday nights. Our total number of meetings is certainly over 1200 — any challengers?
>
> "I've been the primary picker of readings all these years, and it's been a heavy burden — what incredible piles of trash I've sorted through to find the gems worthy of us!
>
> "Of our most-read authors Alice Munro wins by a large margin. Why? Read her and you will know. In second place is V.S. Pritchett. Individual stories also get repeated: "Sorrow — Acre" by Isak Dinesen, "The Real Thing" by Henry James and three times, by request, "In Dreams Begin Responsibilities" by Delmore Schwartz."

Stitch Lasting Friendships With Texture By Weaving Yourself Into a Quilting Bee

Maybe it was the movie "How To Make an American Quilt" with Winona Ryder.

Or maybe it was the overwhelming compassion and meaning reflected in the scores of quilts covering 16 football fields in the AIDS Memorial Quilt.

Whatever the reason, the popularity of "quilting bees" or "quilting circles" has threaded its way back into a revived American tradition that's not only therapeutic, creative and social but it's also stress-reducing too. The heart rate drops by about 11 beats per minute in experienced needle workers (New York University Medical Center).

There are now 14 million quilting households in the U.S., according to the First National Survey of Quilting in America in 1994. One quilting bee in Kannapolis, NC won national recognition (and $2000) from the "Make A Difference Day" campaign for making 60 quilts for 60 premature babies.

So if you're the needling type and you love texture, color, geometry, making statements and making friends, then consider joining one of the over 200 active quilting bees, chapters, circles or guilds throughout the U.S.

For more information, contact The National Quilting Association, Inc. P.O. Box 393, Ellicott City, MD 21041 or call 410-461-5733. Or contact *Quilter's Newsletter Magazine***, P.O. Box 59021, Boulder, CO 80322 or call 303-604-1464.**

Donate Your Baby's Cord Blood And Greatly Raise Expectations Of Bone Marrow Transplants

"About 40% of the desperately ill patients who need bone marrow transplants never get them, because a donor who is an exact match can't be found through family connections or by the National Marrow Donor Program," reported *The Harvard Health Letter* in its March, 1997 issue.

"Two reports in the July 18, 1996 *New England Journal of Medicine* strongly suggest that many of these patients could be helped by transplants of stem cells from placental blood — which is routinely discarded after babies are delivered."

Like bone marrow, the stem cells in a baby's cord blood and the mother's placenta are rich in their power to generate healthy red blood cells, white blood cells and platelets.

By capturing this potent blood fertilizer at birth and banking it for years at the University of Arizona, doctors can use it to replace destroyed or diseased stem cells of patients who were awaiting bone marrow transplants. These include cancer patients with leukemia, lymphoma, myeloma and neuroblastoma or patients who have any of 12 other blood, gene or immunological disorders.

Worldwide, there have been approximately 500 cord blood transplants performed as of March, 1997.

If parents donate their baby's cord blood to help speed a potential bone marrow match, there is no charge. However if parents elect to bank the blood as insurance against a future need by their child or family members, then they or their health provider pay a fee. Either way, the process needs to begin 60 days before the due date.

In the meantime, everyone in the baby chain — obstetricians, pediatricians, nurses, hospitals, mid-wives, baby food processors like Gerber's, baby clothes manufacturers, etc. — should all pull together to get the word out to parents who not only are bringing new life into the world but also can now be giving a new lease on life to someone in need.

For more information, contact the Cord Blood Registry, 1200 Bayhill Dr., Ste. 301, San Bruno, CA 94066; call 888-CORD BLOOD or visit their website at http://www.cordblood.com.

"Educate The Children Foundation"
Create Educational Parity
By Recycling Textbooks & Technology

A common sense solution so obvious, one wonders how such a propitious re-distribution could be overlooked for so many years.

Just like Second Harvest and America Harvest collect excess food from banquets, movie premieres and restaurants and distribute it to those less fortunate, Educate The Children Foundation is a national roundhouse for  recycling overstocked school books and magazines from publishers; refurbishing classroom furniture; acquiring and installing educational software and hardware and delivering these critical supplies to underfunded school districts.

Citing the "massive problem" of children who are "like an anchor that's stuck dragging the country back," retirees Frank Clarke and his wife, Faye, started their nonprofit Educate The Children Foundation in 1991 with a portion of their retirement fund. They have since collected and re-distributed over $15 million in educational materials and technology to schools in Alabama, Arkansas, California, Georgia, Ohio, Louisiana, Mississippi, Tennessee and South Dakota as well as in Ghana, Jamaica, Haiti and the U.S. Virgin Islands. This extraordinary couple earned the President's Service Award in 1996 and the prestigious National Caring Award in 1997.

Yet in this land of plenty but unequal distribution, the Foundation is in need of an expanded corps of retired school teachers and educators, concerned individuals and corporations, delivery networks and enlightened suppliers to truly even the scales of public education throughout the U.S.

For more information, contact Educate The Children Foundation, 5862 Bolsa Ave., Ste. 108, Huntington Beach, CA 92649; call 714-901-7237 or visit their website at http://www.etcf.org.

"Break Away"
Replace "Where The Girls Are" With "Where The Community Service Projects Are"

Talk about toppling a treasured tradition!

Spring Break — the great annual lemming migration of hundreds of thousands of college students jamming into cars and driving nonstop to Ft. Lauderdale, the coast of Texas or Palm Springs — is being moderately challenged with a thoughtful alternative known as "Break Away."

Created at Vanderbilt University in 1991, Break Away: the Alternative Break Connection is a national organization that provides leadership training for students who want to organize community service projects during their school breaks. The community organizations get a much-needed jolt of youthful activism and, in turn, students get to contribute to worthy projects in distant communities.

Sample projects have included students from Western Michigan and Grand Valley State working at an endangered animal sanctuary; students from UNC - Chapel Hill renovating low-income housing; students from Western Washington working at 4 hunger sites and students from the University of San Diego spending a week at a new charter school in Phoenix among dozens of others.

Although there are Break Away chapters at over 35 colleges and universities across the U.S., there are 100s more that could easily implement this meaningful alternative to the mobile mayhem that may be fun once but becomes empty with repetition.

For information on starting a chapter at your school —or coaxing your son or daughter to start one — contact Break Away, 6026 Station B, Nashville, TN 37235; call 615-343-0385 or visit their website at http://www.vanderbilt.edu/breakaway/cbab.html.

=========

Another neat college community service group to contact is COOL.

Designed to empower college students to strengthen the nation through community service, Campus Outreach Opportunity League is a national nonprofit that has leadership programs and models to help students create community solutions.

For more information, contact COOL, 1511 K Street, NW, Ste. 307, Washington, DC 20005; call 202-637-7004 or visit their website at http://www.COOL2SERVE.org.

CHAPTER 14

Digging In For Earth & Wildlife

Individual

INDIVIDUAL #21

WWF's "Living Planet Campaign"
Help Draw a Line Around The World's Top 200 Ecoregions

Hailed as "the most comprehensive strategy to date for the conservation of the natural world" by leading scientist Dr. Edward O. Wilson, the World Wildlife Fund's "Living Planet Campaign" identifies the world's top 200 ecoregions that need protection from climate change, deforestation, overfishing, poachers and polluters.

The most aggressive effort in the organization's 25-year history to collectively create a turning point in the conservation movement, this campaign is designed "to mobilize and guide those who can make a difference in conservation, from world leaders to the average citizen,"

defined Kathryn S. Fuller, president of the World Wildlife Fund.

"If we can conserve the broadest variety of the world's habitats, we can conserve the broadest variety of the world's species, as well as the ecological and evolutionary processes that maintain the diversity of nature."

A parallel effort by the WWF annually exposes the 10 most endangered animal and plant species that need accelerated attention despite national and international protection laws.

Alphabetically, the top 10 include:

- Alligator Snapping Turtle
- Beluga Sturgeon
- Big Leaf Mahogany
- Black Rhino (Less than 2500)
- Giant Panda (Less than 1000)
- Golden Seal
- Green-Cheeked Parrot
- Hawksbill Sea Turtle
- Mako Shark
- Tiger (Less than 6000)

To join WWF's urgent ecoregion and endangered species campaigns, contact World Wildlife Fund, 1250 Twenty-Fourth St., NW, Washington, DC 20037; call 202-293-4800 or visit their website at http://www.worldwildlife.org.

========

For years, people have scoffed at the "Save the Whales" campaign and other "Treehugger" types whose mission is to educate people on why we must change our ways.

Except for the tactics of some extremist groups, they're right on target. We must set up a defense against the loss of animal and plant species because if they become extinct, so could our grandchildren's children. In fact, *25% of the world's species of mammals are threatened with extinction, and about half of those may be gone in a decade.*

To learn more on how to keep the precious trilogy of humans, wildlife and the environment in balance, here are just a few of the ways to get involved online:

- **EcoNet** at **http://www.igc.org/igc/issues/habitats**
- **Envirolink** at **http://www.envirolink.org/issues/esa**
- **National Wildlife Federation** at **http://www.nwf.org/**
- **U.S. Fish and Wildlife Service** at **http://www.fws.gov**

The above websites have "links" to multiple grass roots organizations, research, lists of endangered species state-by-state and access to documents such as the Endangered Species Act.

"The Ocean Wildlife Campaign"
Turn The Tide
On Unprecedented Low Fish Populations

Since oceans seem endless, we falsely assume its resident populations are endless too.

Just the opposite. In 1997, populations of fish are at historic lows. For example:

- Atlantic Sea Scallops are overfished
- Black Sea Bass are overfished
- Blue and White Marlin are down 60% to 80%
- Lemon Sole is at a near record low
- Monkfish are overfished
- Red Snapper is seriously depleted
- Some Shark species are down 80%
- Some Tuna species are down as much as 90%
- Swordfish are down 70%

If these disturbing trends aren't reversed and stabilized within the next several years, then there will be one huge wipeout of the world's most important commercial fish.

A convergence of culprits has brought us to the brink. These include unrestricted overfishing; undeterred "bycatching" where 25% of the world's total catch is unintentionally killed and tossed dead back into the sea; habitat destruction; pollution and poor, or simply, nonexistent management.

The problems are so serious a coalition of *six* conservation groups — National Audubon Society, National Coalition for Marine Conservation, Natural Resources Defense Council, New England Aquarium, Wildlife Conservation Society and World Wildlife Fund — have drawn a proverbial line in the sea by mounting "The Ocean Wildlife Campaign" to create efficiencies in mass education; legal resources; lobbying for policy changes and

putting pressure on the commercial fishing industry.

Some of their efforts are paying off. On January 1, 1998, new federal regulations require commercial fishing to reduce by up to 65% of its catch of 83 species of ground fish. In addition, 25 restaurants in New York and Texas voluntarily imposed a 1-year moratorium on serving swordfish. That's a start but there needs to be much more conservation and education.

To help turn the tide, contact The Ocean Wildlife Campaign, 1901 Pennsylvania Ave., NW, Ste. 1100, Washington, DC 20006; call 202-861-2242 or visit their website at http://www.audubon.org/campaign/lo/ow.

(The logo is the property of the Ocean Wildlife Campaign and is used with permission.)

"Great American Fish Count"
Although Divers Do It Deeper,
Now They Can Also Be Census Takers

Recreation with a porpoise ... and a purpose!

Divers who are passionate about preserving the precious aquatic life that sustains their sport should also consider joining the nationwide "Great American Fish Count." (GAFC)

 Marine biologists and scientists are hampered by a lack of fresh research and fish count data to better manage fisheries for current and future generations. Now there's a way to accelerate the learning curve.

Organized similar to a Census Bureau, GAFC has 2 basic needs: Quantity and Species.

Don't worry — you don't have to be an expert and know the difference between a rockfish and a surfperch — as identification seminars are held prior to the surveys. However you are expected to thoroughly cover your "dive neighborhood;" transfer the data on your waterproof survey to a 4-page form and return it in a timely fashion.

While it's been conducted annually for 2 weeks every summer since 1992, the GAFC and a host of cooperating organizations also need ongoing fish counts throughout the year.

Divers and snorkelers concentrate their fish-sighting efforts in National Marine Sanctuary communities which include Channel Islands and Monterey Bay in California, Flower Garden Banks in Texas, Gray's Reef in Georgia, the Florida Keys and many other locations around the U.S.

With 5 organizations collaborating — American Oceans Campaign, Channel Islands National Park, National Oceanic and Atmospheric Administration's National Marine Sanctuary Program, Reef Environmental Education Foundation and the Marine Conservation Network — divers receive a grateful reception for their valuable volunteer research and are introduced to a dedicated corps of individuals who are committed to preserving the quality of our oceans and the denizens of the deep.

To dive in, contact the Great American Fish Count, Channel Islands National Marine Sanctuary, 113 Harbor Way, Santa Barbara, CA 93109; call 805-966-7107 or visit their website at http:// www.cinms.nos.noaa.gov/.

"Volunteer Vacations"
On Your Next Trip,
Be an Environmental Intern

Had enough surprises at a Holiday Inn?

Want to actually *do* something on your vacation and create your own "Wild Discovery" experience?

Then consider a "Volunteer Vacation" where you can be an environmental intern working on any number of fascinating and challenging excursions all over the world.

Projects range from clearing hiking trails to hosting a campground; monitoring alligator egg hatchlings; renovating ancient temples; finding hieroglyphic etchings in the bush; counting songbirds to building a village.

To start, get a copy of *Volunteer Vacations* by Bill McMillon. It cross-references over 150 organizations offering learning programs by cost, length, location, season and whether it's environmental, ecological, cultural, scientific or humanitarian.

Also keep in mind that some of these vacations are tax deductible as well. So you can reduce your gross income and invest in planet Earth at the same time.

For information on ordering the book, contact Chicago Review Press, 814 N. Franklin St., Chicago, IL 60610 or call 312-337-0747.

"The Nature Conservancy"
If We Financially Own The Environment, We Can Responsibly Control Its Fate ... Here's Where You Can Do Both

Oil companies like ARCO and Shell assure long-term growth by *owning* huge oil fields.

Paper companies like Potlach and Weyerhauser assure long-term growth by *owning* forests.

Just like these successful companies that control blocks of the environment, The Nature Conservancy helps to assure a line of protection around our house-of-cards ecosystem by first *owning* deserts, foothills, islands, marshes, prairies, swamps and wetlands that are natural sanctuaries and habitats to endangered plants and animals and then managing them with the most sophisticated preservation techniques.

Currently, The Nature Conservancy owns 1500 preserves comprising 10 million acres throughout the U.S; over 60 million acres in Central and South America and the Caribbean and the Conservancy's Asia Program is expanding to 5 countries in the South Pacific.

Using low-profile, non-political, scientific strategies, The Nature Conservancy was the only environmental organization rated as one of the 10 most effective nonprofits in the U.S. by *MONEY* magazine.

Despite its abundant successes since 1950, the Conservancy has an even more urgent challenge since the U.S. government has systematically reduced its purchases of land for preservation over the last 5 years. Naturally that means developers have one less competitor for buying precious land.

Today, The Nature Conservancy needs individuals who can get out on the front lines by volunteering at its nationwide chapters. Here are just a few of the ways members have personally made their mark on the land:

- 550 trumpeter swans were saved when the Snake River unexpectedly froze in Idaho.

- 100 acres of rare valley oaks were replanted in California.

- 300 bison were released on the Tallgrass Prairie Preserve in Oklahoma.

So if you have a nose for business and a heart for animals and the environment, join The Nature Conservancy and become a true global force of over 900,000 members.

For more information, contact The Nature Conservancy, 1815 North Lynn St., Arlington, VA 22209; call 800-628-6860 or visit their website at http://www.tnc.org.

"Rails-To-Trails Conservancy"
Blaze New Paths By Converting Abandoned Rail Lines

While it's the end of the line for 3000-4000 miles of railroad track each year, it's a new beginning for community-spirited hikers, bikers, equestrians, in-line skaters, crosscountry skiers and habitat homesteaders who want to prevent abandoned rail lines from being permanently parceled off to developers and instead transformed into "linear parks" and trails.

A step-by-step catalyst that professionally guides people into local action is the Rails-To-Trails Conservancy (RTC) which not only acts as a complete information roundhouse but also as a "short-term intermediary between railroad companies and trail groups or public agencies."

In 1987 — when RTC opened — there were 90 rail-trails. Today there are 918 with 1000 more in the works. Yet much more track needs to be unlaid and re-made.

Besides the recreational benefits, rail-trails can have a significant economic benefit. For example:

- The Bike Stop served 1800 customers on a single day because of Boston's Minuteman Trail.

- Woodworker Karl Koenig now has a mailing list of 100,000 since the Katy Trail went through his backyard in Defiance, MO.

Through its nationwide networks, RTC can provide technical assistance to individuals as well as local planners who want to start new trails to run through their hometowns. To that end, RTC publishes several helpful guides such as *Secrets of Successful Rail-Trails: An Acquisition and Organizing Manual for Converting Rails into Trails* ($19.95).

For more information, contact Rails-To-Trails Conservancy, 1100 Seventeenth St., NW, 10th Floor, Washington, DC 20036; call 202-331-9696 or visit their website at http://www. railtrails.org.

"Coastal Cookbook"
Reclaim Our Shorelines With 49 Recipes

If you want to do something at the beach besides building another sandcastle and then later getting the moat all over your floor mats, consider getting a free copy of the Environmental Protection Agency's *Coastal Cookbook.*

In 1993, research firm Horsley & Witten, Inc. placed a "call for recipes" of creative programs preserving coastal beaches and marshes that lap up on 22 states from Maine to California.

From 100s submitted, they selected the best 49 and then made them reader-friendly. Their clear distillations show you how to adapt one or several of these recipes to your coastal community.

Here's a sample:

- Citizen Pollution Reporting System
- Fish Net Collection
- Marsh Terracing
- Officer Snook Marine Project
- Protecting Sand Dunes
- Sanctuary Watch
- Shorewatch Video
- Wetlands Restoration

For your free copy, request EPA document 842-F-94-002 subtitled *Innovations In Coastal Protection: Searching For Uncommon Solutions To Common Problems,* EPA, 401 M St., SW (4504F), Washington, DC 20460 or call 202-260-1952.

Be a "Backyard Bird Counter" And Join America's Fastest-Growing Outdoor Activity

Calling all "Backyard Bird Counters" who regularly feed their feathered friends and now want to feed important data into a national citizen-science study.

Called Project FeederWatch, the program requests individuals from all across North America to record only the numbers and kinds of birds who feed at your bird feeder over a 2-week period from November to March.

Your observations are then compiled into a national study to detect significant population declines before a species approaches extinction.

Coordinated by the Cornell Lab of Ornithology, other citizen-science projects include:

- Birds in Forested Landscapes
- Cornell Nest Box Network
- House Finch Disease Survey
- Project Pigeon Watch

Cost to join the Project FeederWatch is $15 which covers the instruction packet; bird ID poster and *Birdscope*, a quarterly newsletter showing results of surveys and the latest articles on bird behavior.

According to *An America Challenged*, bird watching is the fastest-growing outdoor activity with a 58% growth rate predicted by the year 2050. Now's the time to get ahead of the curve.

For more information, contact Project FeederWatch/PFW, Cornell Lab of Ornithology, P.O. Box 11, Ithaca, NY 14851; call 800-843-BIRD or visit their website at http://www.ornith. cornell.edu.

========

"Christmas Bird Count"
Or Join Audubon's
Annual Audit For Wildlife

The longest-running wildlife survey is National Audubon's "Christmas Bird Count" where over 46,000 people participate by taking about 1700 bird counts during a 2-week period every December.

For more information, contact National Audubon Society, 700 Broadway, New York, NY 10003; call 212-979-3000 or visit their website at http://www.audubon.org/bird/cbc/index.html.

"Plant a Tree a Year For Life"
Your Immortality Will Be Guaranteed

Community volunteers seeking to make a lasting statement for themselves and planet Earth should consider contacting the American Free Tree Program (AFTP).

Founded in 1989, the AFTP project — whose theme is "Plant a Tree a Year For Life" — is so practical and in line for keeping the precious balance of nature for future generations.

Ideally, hometown volunteers are sought to rally local tree troops and make it a community-wide event, year after year. A Training Manual is available for $25 to steer and organize volunteers or civic groups into conducting tree-planting days.

AFTP now has 119 countywide free tree projects in 9 states. Its goal is to form an international network of 5000 community volunteer projects to buy, distribute, plant and maintain 1 billion trees in North America.

To make a lasting memory in your hometown, contact American Free Tree Program, Inc. P.O. Box 9079, Canton, OH 44711 or call 330-454-3111.

CHAPTER 15

20-Point
Front-End Alignment

Individual

INDIVIDUAL #30

"Happiness For Dummies"
Only Requires 2 Rules

Despite popular belief, happiness does not come with a new car, a new home or a new job.

To build a lifelong habit for happiness, consider the 2 most frequently cited changes you can make in your life.

They are:

- **Taking Control Of Your Life**
- **Having Close Personal Relationships**

When Scott Adams — the creator of the loopy "Dilbert" cartoon strip — was idling away at PacBell for 17 years, he decided to take more control of his life via a focused meditation he put down on paper everyday.

"The basic idea," he stated in *Newsweek*, "is that 15 times a day, you just write down whatever it is your goal is." So 15 times a day, he wrote I WILL BECOME A SYNDICATED CARTOONIST and started sending his samples out. Among all the rejections was an acceptance from United Feature Syndicate. Today his depiction of cubicle life twisted by dorky bosses espousing the latest absurd management babble is a runaway hit as it appears in 1100 newspapers.

"Having a strong sense of controlling one's life is a more dependable predictor of positive feelings of well-being than any of the objective conditions of life we considered," observed Angus Campbell who was the researcher of 170,000 people surveyed in *The Pursuit of Happiness*.

The other pillar for building a basic foundation is cementing strong and faithful personal relationships. Probably not earth-shattering news but a mountain of evidence says that the strength and depth of our relationships, not the multiplicity of relations will increase our overall happiness.

"The most important factor in happiness is good interpersonal relations — with friends, family, lovers, etc.," unequivocally stated Alex C. Michalos, Ph.D. who conducted a survey of 18,000 undergraduate students in 39 countries.

"They (interpersonal relations) contribute the biggest bang in terms of happiness and are much more important than looks or income."

Widen Your Emotional Bandwidth

Feel overwhelmed by the incessant flow and quantity of information?

Feel unnoticed because your letters, Post-It Notes, e-mails, projects, brochures, slide shows and even phone calls are not getting attention?

Feel numbed because computers and information technology are too cold, analytical and seemingly anti-human?

Then it's time to "make room for the new way of doing business," wrote Stan Davis in *Forbes* magazine.

"Information technologies are going to make emotions a regular feature. Why? The more information becomes an infinite resource, the more attention becomes a scarce resource. And the best way to get attention is through emotions.

"Emotional bandwidth will become an enabling technology that will manifest itself in software, in interfaces, in search engines, on Web pages and in computer and communications architectures," summarized Davis who is also the author of *Future Perfect*.

"It's coming from the most unemotional of disciplines, engineering, and it is being built into the entire range of information technologies. As this happens, silicon will enable us to express more completely who we are, as people and as businesses."

So constructively siphon off some of those bottled-up emotions and artfully polish them into your paper and e-mail communications to be seen and heard above the masses both today … and into the 21st Century.

Listen Without Importing

*"No man would listen if he didn't
know it was his turn next."*

— Ed Howe

How many times have you been in conversation with someone on a string of topics and invariably — whenever you bring up a new topic — the other person immediately launches into his or her personal take which of course instantly shifts the focus off your original topic?

It's infuriating to the point of grating. For example:

You: "Well, my daughter finally got a B in Math."

Other Person: "Spencer is doing great; he got an A in Algebra, B in English and I almost died when he got an A in Spanish. His Spanish teacher, Mr. Mendoza, is so weird. I mean how did he get his teacher's certificate? Yada, yada, yada."

Since we have become so self-centered about the issues and people around us, we subconsciously close doors to learning by always importing our trivial trail without truly listening in conversations.

In addition, men who interrupt and take control of conversations are 60% more likely to die during the next 22 years according to a 1997 study of 700 men at the Duke University Medical Center.

Civility in society and personal development would leap ahead if we could just withhold our need to immediately expound and listen without interjecting every little personal nook and nuance onto someone else's stage.

Or as Epictetus said some 2000 years ago: "We have two ears and one mouth and should use them in that proportion."

Better Your Friendships
By Risking Them

In a culture that fosters façades and denies true feelings, who is devoting the energy to the arduous process of rubbing together the sticks of time and honesty to create the lasting fire of friendship?

While Artistotle described friendship as a single soul dwelling in 2 bodies, today friendship has often taken on a hollow definition in this self-centered, isolated, high tech and frequently frosty world.

Relationships are often disguised as friendships, yet sometimes they are outright manipulations; casual acquaintances in lieu of true, soul-baring friendships. Unfortunately, in an age when people do more colliding than connecting, these "friendships in disguise" are quite common.

"You want a friend in life, get a dog," former U.S. President Harry S. Truman once said. A cynical New Yorker says, "A friend in need is no friend of mine;" a comic gets a laugh with his admission that "I have friends I haven't used yet" and a public relations executive clings to some homespun advice: "I do what Mom said: 'Make friends when you don't need them.'"

Yet — despite the tendency for the critical mass to devalue the importance of friendships — for those who have developed a close cluster of friends and who want to strengthen those bonds there are a few points to keep in mind.

Real friendship *demands* and *insists* on total and mutual honesty. Anything less reduces a friendship to a shallow and less fulfilling relationship. Honesty stops manipulation when one person is bent on pleasing the other; when one uses the other for an undisclosed purpose or when one leans on the other to make up for his or her deficiencies.

Real friends go beyond what is expected of each other; they do as much as they can for each other, asking nothing in return.

Real friendship also grows at a natural rate, never hurried or forced, but always pressing for higher levels of personal exchange. It will even press to the point of risking that friendship to snap a friend out of blind denial — or telling that friend something he or she doesn't want to hear but needs to hear — making sure that the friend's best interests are at the heart of the brutal revelation or raw recommendation. Tough stuff, but well worth it.

Look Out For The Person
Who's *Not* Looking Out For You!

On July 14, 1992, my 15-year-old daughter, Jessica, lay in a coma in the emergency room of a hospital. A web of wires was hooked from her body to a wall monitor showing signs of life but not much else. The gut-wrenching emotion and singular concentration of those ticking moments while waiting for someone, anyone to appear are ever so vivid.

Then suddenly an orderly came in and said, "We're going to do a CAT-scan." He immediately started to wheel her bed out of the tiny cubicle but neglected to unhook the wires.

"Hey, she's still hooked up!" I yelled. Sheepishly, he apologized and carefully unhooked her. Later I found out it was the end of his shift and he was anxious to hit the freeway.

Although Jessica miraculously recovered from having a sub-arachnoid aneurysm, I learned a valuable lesson.

No matter where we are, we as individuals will more and more have to "over think" for the person who's not looking out for us.

How many times have you heard of parents leaving the hospital with someone else's baby? In Riverside, CA, a couple was told by a doctor that the twins they were expecting had a rare disease and would be deformed. Advised by a friend, the mother went on the Internet and learned of a new treatment the doctor wasn't aware of. It was performed and the parents had healthy twins. In another case, a doctor mistakenly amputated the wrong leg of a patient.

It's not only in hospitals but it happens ever more frequently on the road with mentally lazy drivers. It's also in offices where people enter incorrect information on health insurance forms, prescriptions, credit reports, bank statements and wherever else seemingly insignificant details are frequently overlooked.

Most people have short attention spans and are thinking about 5 or 6 other things *except* the immediate, tedious task at hand, i.e. what's critically important to you. So prepare for the person who's not looking out for you and it'll save you in countless ways throughout life.

Watch What You Say ...
The Subconscious Can't Take a Joke!

"The subconscious mind is the storehouse of total memory, seed of habit, the seat of intuition and the faithful servant that takes 'orders' from the conscious mind," wrote Marilyn Jenett in the *Century City Chronicle*.

"The subconscious accepts suggestion through the spoken word, inner thoughts and outside influences, and once impregnated with a suggestion, will automatically and compulsively act on that idea to manifest the end result. The subconscious does not have the ability to make judgments and does not reason whether this result is positive or negative. It merely acts on the given command to ensure its fulfillment. The same neutral mental power that produces the good in your life also produces that which is not good.

"Every word we speak, every thought we think, and every emotion we feel is recorded in the subconscious. Through repetition or with enough faith or emotional impact, the subconscious will accept our words as a command and will create subjectively and also attract and magnetize circumstances, conditions and persons to ensure the manifestation of our 'order.'

"Even words spoken casually can bypass the conscious mind and drop into the subconscious and take root. It has been said that the subconscious can't take a joke. Seemingly harmless expressions can produce undesirable results in our lives.

"On the other hand, positive, life-enhancing words will produce results after their kind and can bring about astonishing results and turn situations around dramatically.

"It's vitally important to monitor the words we use. We must become aware of the impact of the words we are saying and thinking (self-talk is just as powerful) as these words create our intent, our mood, our ability to attract and repel, the story and very fabric of our lives."

(Marilyn Jenett is the owner of a special event location and production company in Century City, CA.)

Peel Away Perception From Reality

Falling prey to prevailing perception over reality can lead to bad decision-making.

When we accept the "perception" of a person or the "perception" of an issue over the reality, it can be disastrous.

Yet accepting an immediate perception today is so pervasive because people are impatient and don't take the extra time to go beyond the path of least resistance. When we make a snap decision by accepting perception over reality, it can often backfire on us.

Surprisingly, we reject reality when it comes to abstract summaries. Although crime statistics are down, people's perceptions are not. Although a 1997 book called *Time for Life* says we have more leisure time than we did 30 years ago, people's perceptions don't agree. Although a study by the Foundation for Clean Air Progress says air pollutants have dropped dramatically since 1970, 58% of Americans believe air quality is getting worse.

To not be fooled by false perceptions and be more heads up on the reality of trends, keep in mind these tips to develop a more perceptive mind's eye to the world:

- Adopt a child-like innocence
- Assume nothing
- Delay judgment when possible
- Discount conventional wisdom
- Eliminate the ego "I" out of decision-making ... see the world as it is, not as you perceive it to be
- Force yourself to be empathetic
- Investigate, Investigate, Investigate
- Practice crystal clear communications

Be The Hit Of Every Party
By Remembering Everybody's Name!

It's time to stop bad-mouthing your memory.

Becoming more and more "absent-minded" is not a growing malady. Actually, the mind is simply absent when people forget. The cure is to bear down and concentrate on paying more attention and then creatively "lock in" connections to specific items you want to remember. It only takes a few extra seconds.

The first step toward improving your memory chip is recognizing that it's not automatic; it's a learned skill just like your, uh, golf game.

"Memory can be divided into two aspects: retention and recall," wrote Tony Buzan in *Make the Most of Your Mind*. "Retention is the ability ... to take in and store information. Recall is the ability to select from that vast store the special piece of information we need at any given time."

Memory then is making that instant connection between retention and recall. It's done with a mnemonic ... connecting something you're unfamiliar with (a new name) with something you're familiar with.

Here are 5 ways to remember names at the next party:

- Create a rhyme ... Sally Shore is a bore.
- Flatter the new person ... ask him or her to repeat their name out loud.
- Make a silly connection ... Robinson ... Robs his Son!
- Repeat the name immediately out loud just after you've been introduced.
- Repeat the name silently at points throughout the party.

At the end of the evening — when everyone else has let the alcohol leech their brain cells — you can personally say goodnight by calling everyone by their first and last name.

Talk about making lasting impressions!

Look For Lasting Consideration
As The #1 Building Brick
To All Personal Relationships

"What's the most important ingredient in a relationship between a man and a woman?" asked Joyce Gabriel in an article in *The Stamford Advocate*.

"A friend of mine came up with one of the best answers I've ever heard, one her grandmother passed on to her.

"It's consideration.

"I was struck by the trueness of this bit of simple philosophy. Consideration should be at the base of all close relationships, but it's especially important between spouses.

"This is a tricky world we live in for a gentle kind of love. Lust is so often offered up instead, as if urgency were the only standard by which to judge the depth of one's feelings. It's a world in which old-fashioned values of kindness and consideration need rekindling.

"It reminded me of something my mother said right after my father died.

"'Who will tell me I'm pretty anymore?' she asked me. 'Even the day before he died, he looked at me and told me how beautiful my hair was.' My dad had still seen her as his pretty wife, had still been considerate enough to pay her a compliment, to want her to bask in his praise.

"Consideration may very well be the key to love that nurtures and love that lasts. When people can share that kind of love, it gives them the strength to get through life."

(Joyce Gabriel is at Newsday *and granted permission to reprint the essence of her article.)*

Never Feel Alone Again!
1000+ Self-Help Groups
Offer Kind Words & Knowing Advice

Think you need some help? Or know someone who does?
But you think that need is too obscure?
Think again …
There are now over 1000 self-help groups offering emotional support
and concrete advice on how to weave through nearly every known problem,
disorder, mental or physical condition.

Here's just a sample of the obscure and not-so-obscure self-help groups
that are ready to reach out:

Agoraphobia	Facial Paralysis
Alzheimer's	Gaucher Disease
Apnea	Graves Disease
Bell's Palsy	Hepatitis
Caregivers	Latex Allergies
Chromosome Disorders	Lupus
Dancing Eye Syndrome	Manic Depression
Emphysema	Stuttering

The American Self-Help Clearinghouse has
contact information on all 1000+ groups in a 270-
page directory; offers a free 2-page sheet on "Ideas
For Starting a Self-Help Group" and software for
helping other clearinghouses develop their databases.

**For more information, contact American Self-
Help Clearinghouse, Northwest Covenant Medical
Center, Denville, NJ 07834; call 973-625-3037 or
visit their website at http://www.cmhc.com/
selfhelp/**

TM

Learn The Fine Print
Of "Face Reading"

Too often people make cursory judgments about someone's personality with only a superficial observation. A look. A smile. A shrug. An irksome comment. Too often these surface clues have no depth for revealing the true personality. But there is a more definitive way to seek the truth.

Physiognomy, or face reading for character evaluation, is an art to which many people only give lip service. There are nearly 200 muscles in our faces. They have been "frozen" into habitual lines and creases by life's daily bombardment of bricks and bouquets — the accumulated years of smiling, expressing, flinching and wincing. Our countenances have been emotionally chiseled into very distinct and readable parts, or chapters, that reveal many of our true attitudes and personalities.

Studying the fine print of a person's face gives a new dimension to understanding the prism of personality.

Face reading can help us predict the character of a potential employee, business partner or new client; re-evaluate a prospective husband or wife and also give us reciprocal insight into our own self-awareness to understand how people subconsciously view us.

For example:

- **Cheeks** … Hollow and angular cheeks can mean suppressed anger or resentment.

- **Crow's Feet** … If they point upward, it usually indicates a person whose smile is genuine while downward lines indicate general sadness. If the crow's feet fan out in all directions, like the rays of the sun, this suggests a warm person who displays emotions openly and frequently.

- **Eyes** … Wide-open eyes denote someone who is very information-oriented and wants his or her emotions conveyed.

- **False Smile** … Slight furrowing of the muscles between the eyebrows which is at odds with the purported expression of pleasure.

- **Forced Smile** ... Actors and politicians often have long, deeply entrenched smile lines that act as parentheses to both sides of the mouth. (Jimmy Carter)

- **Lips** ... Thin or narrow lips are often associated with angry, stubborn or constrictive characteristics. Full lips are the sign of a sensuous person; habitual relaxation and one who wishes to be loved but can be devastated by rejection. (Marilyn Monroe)

- **Lips & Mouth** ... Drawn down at the corners can be a sign of chronic irritation. Vertical lines at the corners can reflect a garrulous person.

- **Noses** ... One that twitches and tweaks during conversation can be showing signs of disdain.

- **Spontaneous Smile** ... The cheeks move up and the muscles around the eye tighten, making crow's feet.

No matter whose face you're reading, a more accurate assessment will always be determined from the study of each part in conjunction with the sum of the parts. For example, a smile is not enough. Radiating lines from the eyes should be in harmony with that smile. If they're not, you may be facing a personality whose motives are questionable.

To read a person like a book, become familiar with these nuances to reveal subtle clues about personality that can help you go beyond the "cover" of a person and more accurately foresee which ones are the bombs and which ones are the potential bestsellers.

Discouragement Is The Best Encouragement

"Teaching people to lose is an important part of teaching them how to win," stated Frank Smoll, a University of Washington sports psychologist, in the *Daily News*.

"The so-called failure might be a gift in disguise," added Smoll who teaches coaches and athletes the value and power of losing.

Thankfully, someone is finally putting some sensibility into sports. In essence, Smoll is saying, 'Let go of our obsession to be first in sports.' Understanding where and how we failed — or rising above medical setbacks — can be a window to something larger than the original goal.

Consider how an ailing Ray Kroc flew out to California to sell the McDonald brothers 8 Multimixers for their popular restaurant and ended up starting the McDonald's chain at the age of 52.

"When I flew back to Chicago that fateful day in 1954, I had a freshly signed contract with the McDonald brothers in my briefcase," he wrote in *Grinding It Out*.

"I was a battle-scarred veteran of the business wars, but I was still eager to go into action. I was 52-years-old with diabetes and incipient arthritis. I had lost my gallbladder and most of my thyroid gland in earlier campaigns. But I was convinced the best was still ahead of me."

19 Reasons To Exercise Your Way To a Quality Life

Can you find 90 to 120 minutes a week so you can write the #1 insurance policy to increase your chances of staying healthy the balance of your life?

With the multidimensional benefits of exercise listed below, there is simply no excuse for 60% of the U.S. population to remain sedentary. None. Zilch.

Let alone the personal benefits, think of the reductions in health care costs if just 10% more of society were to take up regular exercise. Regardless of age — from 9 to 90 —mandate exercise into your life today.

Regular Moderate Exercise ...

- Cuts chances of a woman having a stroke or heart attack *in half!*
- Helps reduce the risk of heart disease and heart attacks in men
- Helps reduce the risk of many forms of cancer, especially colon and breast cancer
- Helps reduce risk of intestinal bleeding in older adults
- Protects against onset of diabetes in middle-aged men
- Improves general memory, especially verbal memory
- Raises HDL (good) cholesterol level in blood
- Increases Growth Hormones 150 to 250%
- Helps reduce the risk of osteoporosis
- Helps keep normal body weight
- Helps reduce arthritic pain
- Cuts hearing loss in half
- Lowers blood pressure
- Improves metabolism
- Stimulates creativity
- Stretches longevity
- Reduces headaches
- Increases energy
- Cuts stress

Do Preventive Maintenance On Your Body

Unfortunately we do more preventive maintenance on our cars than we do on our bodies.

Although we steadfastly have regular oil changes every 3000 miles, how many of us have regularly scheduled mammograms or prostate exams among other simple body maintenance procedures?

While we can always get another car, as humans we only come in one make and model.

Although your genetic background, age and lifestyle risk factors will affect your check-up time lines — and there are disagreements within the specialized medical fields as to what is generally appropriate — the following is a flexible schedule designed to stimulate a habit of preventive maintenance.

MEN & WOMEN

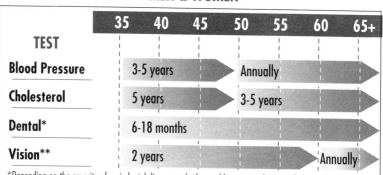

TEST	35	40	45	50	55	60	65+
Blood Pressure	3-5 years			Annually			
Cholesterol	5 years			3-5 years			
Dental*	6-18 months						
Vision**	2 years						Annually

*Depending on the severity of periodontal disease and other problems, your dentist will recommend your call-back timeframe.
**The American Academy of Ophthalmology suggests longer intervals. The American Optometric Assn. recommends routine exams every 2-4 years until age 64, then every 1-2 years.

MEN & WOMEN

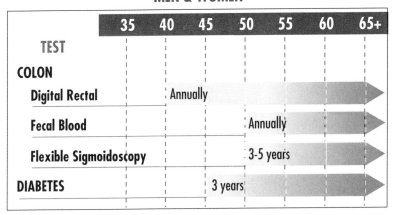

WOMEN

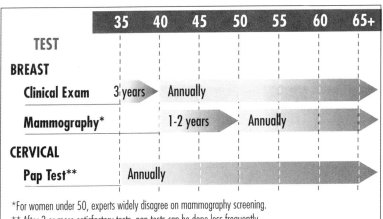

*For women under 50, experts widely disagree on mammography screening.
** After 3 or more satisfactory tests, pap tests can be done less frequently.

MEN

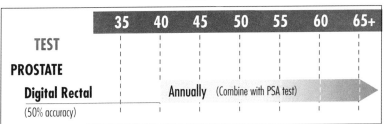

(Chart compiled by national health and fitness journalist Kathleen Doheny of Burbank, CA.)

Preserve Your Health
By Being Less Perfect

Is this you ... or someone you know?

Impatient? "Wrapped tight?" Walks with clenched teeth over the petty errors of others? Incessantly strives to prove one's worth? Micromanages every detail down to the last second or last penny?

If so, consider having or suggesting a "Personality Overhaul" real soon!

According to a report in *Creative Living*, a 10-year study of more than 10,000 managers and professionals by Human Synergistics found that perfectionists were *75% more likely* to have numerous symptoms ranging from headaches and depression to gastrointestinal and cardiovascular complaints.

As the senior author noted, "Perfectionism is a way of thinking and behaving, that on the surface seems a search for excellence ... but actually brings great unhappiness, massive imperfection and poor health."

Or as Sylvia Robinson once said, "Some think that it's holding on that makes one strong. Sometimes it's letting go."

Give The Gift Of Life To Others, Men ... And Potentially Reduce Your Risk Of Heart Disease By Up To 30%

Men's hearts, especially those over 40, are believed to decrease their chances of breakdown if their owners donate blood at the local American Red Cross.

A highly-debated 1997 study tracking 3855 men for 8 years concluded that by donating blood men may reduce their risk of heart disease (hardening of the arteries) by *up to 30%*. However the benefit is negated for men who smoke.

The University of Kansas Medical Center study published in *Heart* supports a previous study in the *British Medical Journal* that reported blood donation reduced the risk of heart attack by 86% among 2682 Finnish men.

Both studies concur on the "iron hypothesis" which says women are generally protected from heart disease because they have lower body stores of iron than men through menstrual flow. The lower amount of iron lessens the chain reaction to cholesterol becoming oxidized. With 50% less iron stores, they believe that's why women have 50% less heart disease than men.

"What this means for men is — if you donate blood, in a sense you can become a virtual woman and protect yourself from heart disease," explained David Meyers, M.D. at the University of Kansas Medical Center. "We have identified another reason for blood donation, beyond altruism, for men."

November through January and June through August are especially critical periods of blood shortages.

Regardless of season, call your local American Red Cross to begin a new protection plan for yourself while starting a new habit for humanity.

"Good Guys Last Longer"
Says 75-Year Study

You have 2 choices at work or home today:

- Be a domineering jerk or ...

- Be an accommodating, cheerful spirit.

If you choose the latter, then you could live 2-4 years longer according to *Creative Living*.

A 75-year study of California school children determined that those who exhibited those corny but core traits of being conscientious, considerate, dependable and honest tacked an extra 2 to 4 years onto their lives.

Although the "good guys" didn't have fewer health problems than their self-centered counterparts in the study, the best explanation for their extended life was their superior ability to handle stress. Impulsive and arrogant men have greater stress which in turn accelerates the aging process.

So pass it on. Dispel the malignant myth of being "lean and mean" and tell younger males it's healthier to chill out because in the long run, "Good Guys Last Longer!"

INDIVIDUAL #47

Discover The Therapeutic Power Of Plants

If you've dismissed plants all your life, rethink them as they can improve your overall health.

Consistent gardening can do wonders such as:

- Control weight
- Improve circulation
- Manage arthritis
- Reduce blood pressure
- Reduce depression
- Reduce stress
- Slow bone loss

"We get dozens of letters a month where people describe how they have been restored either mentally or physically by their garden," reported Mike McGrath, former editor-in-chief at *Organic Gardening*.

"The most dramatic one was from a mother whose 12-year-old daughter was killed by a car in front of their house. The mother went into severe depression for six months.

"By that time, spring came and she hadn't gotten around to canceling her subscription. As she was reading articles that described the joys of planting again, she looked outside and decided that rather than be a source of pain, the garden would be a way to keep her daughter alive since it was an activity they enjoyed together. She wrote to say we had gotten her out of the chair for the first time in six months."

According to McGrath, there's been a tremendous surge in the study of horticultural therapy in recent years. In a study at Kansas State University, the 3 most common measures of stress — blood pressure, heart rate and skin temperature — all decreased within 15 minutes after a group of 20 adults started toiling away in a greenhouse.

So regardless of the color of your thumb, plot that garden and let the good earth sift through your fingers. You'll be tapping into the tonic of better health.

Hold The Joe And Reach For The H_2O ... Liquid Insurance For Smooth Sailing

Although routinely dismissed, drinking lots of water is truly a wonder defense for a healthier cruise through life.

The body's year-round need for water goes way beyond fulfilling a thirst just when it's hot.

Drinking 8-10 cups of water a day lessens fatigue; regulates body temperature; aids digestion; serves as an appetite suppressant and greatly lessens your chances of getting constipation, kidney stones, urinary tract infections, other bladder problems or "dry mouth."

Our net water losses per day are:

2 cups for respiration
2 cups for perspiration
6 cups for kidneys and intestines

10 cups lost everyday

Since most of our daily intake of food only contains about 3.5 cups of water, we easily need those 8-10 cups just to keep our body functioning on an even keel.

Sure, you'll be hopping and skipping to the bathroom a lot more but just think of it as sloshing your way to a continual feeling of well-being. Make it a daily habit and soon your body will scream for another tall cool one!

"It's What You Learn — After You Know It All —That Counts!"
— John Wooden

The arrogance of omniscience is a truly insipid and destructive force in our society.

It permeates every institution in the public and private sector chipping away the spirit and soul of every individual.

Corporate leaders, middle management, rank-and-file employees, politicians, self-appointed pundits, executive directors, entrepreneurs, doctors, educators, students and retirees should learn to embrace the mantra that "Mental vigor is the essence of life" as Senator Jacob Javitz eloquently articulated at the age of 80 even while his body was being ravaged by Lou Gehrig's disease.

While Picasso achieved higher levels of creativity with new styles of painting in his 90s and Georgia O'Keefe won the National Medal of Arts at the tender age of 98, present and future generations will be better served by everyone dropping the presumption of knowing it all; cracking open a few books; reading dozens more magazines; exploring the depths of knowledge imbedded in websites; practicing a habit of lifelong learning and then sharing this new information with employees, clients, patients, students, friends and family … to make it all count.

INDEX

ADDITIONAL PHOTO CREDITS

Roberto Clemente in Dedication *Vintage Sports Photographs*

Back Cover *Photo by Delmar Watson*